THE FOURTH WORLD CONFERENCE
ON FAITH AND ORDER

THE FOURTH
WORLD CONFERENCE ON
FAITH AND ORDER

Montreal 1963

The Report edited by
P. C. RODGER
Executive Secretary, Commission on Faith and Order,
World Council of Churches

and

LUKAS VISCHER
Research Secretary, Commission on Faith and Order,
World Council of Churches

ASSOCIATION PRESS
New York

THE FOURTH WORLD CONFERENCE ON FAITH AND ORDER

© World Council of Churches 1964

First published in the United States, 1964,
by Association Press, 291 Broadway, New York, N.Y. 10007

In preparation for the Fourth World Conference
on Faith and Order, Association Press published

INSTITUTIONALISM AND CHURCH UNITY

Printed in Great Britain
by Billing and Sons Ltd
Guildford and London

CONTENTS

FOREWORD

by Oliver S. Tomkins

Bishop of Bristol and Chairman of the Conference

THE FOURTH World Conference on Faith and Order at Montreal in July 1963 took place under very different circumstances from its predecessors. The Lausanne and Edinburgh conferences were held between the two world wars, before the World Council of Churches was born. Lund in 1952 was the first Faith and Order World Conference within the framework of the World Council, but it laid down the lines on which the Montreal conference was planned.

The chief impression, upon my mind, of this most recent conference was that the ecumenical movement today is so complex, so comprehensive and set amidst such fast-moving events, that our traditional conference method is inadequate for registering its whole range of implications. This report reflects, I believe, both our inadequacy and yet our exhilaration at the causes of it. The time available was too short for the Section Reports to be considered by the whole conference at such depth as to justify their adoption as the report of the whole conference. We commend them to the study of the churches on their intrinsic merit. The facts that Eastern Orthodoxy was represented for the first time in adequate strength, that Roman Catholic observers and guests kept us aware of the open dialogue with Rome, that the churches of Asia, Africa and Latin America were vocally present as never before, that many of our themes cut across confessional lines—all these must be borne in mind in assessing the conference.

The result was described by one delegate as 'a most promising chaos'. The sense of vitality was at once our hope and our despair. The World Council's Faith and Order Commission now faces some searching questions about how we should proceed. But our problems arise out of the abundance of the tasks to be faced, so we thank God for them. Meanwhile, we offer our report to the churches in the prayer that God will use it to bring us all nearer to the one truth which is in Christ.

OLIVER BRISTOL

I

A MONTREAL DIARY

David M. Paton

MONTREAL is one of the main cities of Canada, founded in 1647 by Paul de Chomedey, and today not only a great industrial and commercial metropolis, but a creative centre of ecumenical fellowship between Roman Catholic, Orthodox, Anglican and Protestant.

The World Conference on Faith and Order that convened there on the campus of McGill University on Friday July 12th was the fourth in a series that reached back through Lund in 1952 and Edinburgh in 1937 to the First World Conference on Faith and Order in Lausanne in 1927, and beyond that to the World Missionary Conference in Edinburgh in 1910. There Bishop Charles Brent had been seized with the conviction that practical church cooperation in missions must issue in the search for unity in faith and order, and had inspired the patient work that led in due course to Lausanne.

In 1927, the idea of theological conferences about Christian Unity was new and exciting. The absence of Rome was not surprising, and it was difficult enough for the Orthodox and the Anglicans and the Protestants to understand each other's convictions. But from Lausanne to Edinburgh and after the work proceeded. At Lund with Faith and Order now part of the World Council of Churches, it was proposed to abandon the theological method of listing and analysing the varying beliefs of the churches—the method of 'comparative ecclesiology'—and to seek instead for the common convictions that underlie them. The first fruit of this new method was the New Delhi statement on the nature of the unity we seek. The response of the churches was prompt and grateful. Yet because of the speed of ecumenical development, and the elaboration of direct church-to-church conversations and negotiations about re-union, there have been for some years serious questionings about the role of Faith and Order in the World Council.

The inheritance of Faith and Order; the changing ecumenical situation; the fact of the whole World Council of Churches; and the pressure on the churches of the world at large in the year of our Lord 1963—these were the background to the Fourth World Conference on Faith and Order. They figured prominently in the opening addresses to the

Conference, and they recurred again and again in its proceedings.

I. THE CONFERENCE BEGINS ITS WORK

The Opening Service The Conference opened in the Winter Stadium of the University with a service of worship conducted by Dr Douglas Horton (United Church of Christ, U.S.A.), Dr Anders Nygren (Church of Sweden), and the Rev. John Gatu (Presbyterian Church of East Africa). The theme of this service was that of the Good Shepherd who gathers together the scattered people of God and gives himself to those who call upon him. The theme was declared in the lessons: Ezek. 34.1-16; John 10.11-18 and 14.23-26; and Luke 11.9-13. The Conference made grateful response in the saying of Psalm 98 and of the Creed, and in the singing of 'Praise to the Lord, the Almighty, the King of Creation', a French version of Psalm 42, and 'Love Divine, all Loves Excelling'. Prayers of thanksgiving, and repentance, and for the presence of the Holy Spirit were concluded with the corporate recital of the New Delhi words of commitment:

> We confess Jesus Christ, Saviour of men and the light of the world;
> Together we accept his command;
> We commit ourselves anew to bear witness to him among men;
> We offer ourselves to serve all men in love, that love which he alone
> imparts;
> We accept afresh our calling to make visible our unity in him.
> We pray for the gift of the Holy Spirit for our task.

The Opening Addresses After the service, the Conference convened in General Session for an address on 'The Ecumenical Situation' by Professor Roger Mehl (Reformed Church of Alsace and Lorraine).[1] Dr Mehl drew attention to four new events in the ecumenical movement which had helped to create the context in which the Montreal Conference met. The first of these events was the adoption at New Delhi of the statement on the nature of the unity we seek and of the fuller and more precise Basis. The World Council was no longer simply a neutral meeting place for dialogue and cooperation between the churches. Its very existence challenged them with a question: 'Can a church today manifest the ecumenical dimension of its message *without* joining the community of churches which is the World Council of Churches?'

The second event was that the Roman Catholic Church, so far as could be judged at present, had realized the necessity of participating in the ecumenical dialogue. 'In the presence of our brethren from the Roman Catholic Church who are here as observers, whom we welcome here as brothers, we should like to say that the churches belonging to

---

[1] For the full text of this address see *The Ecumenical Review*, October 1963, pp. 1-13.

the World Council do not regard the Vatican Council as an event which does not concern them, but as an event which affects them all because it really concerns the history of the true universal church. . . .' With equal frankness Dr Mehl went on to recall the basic conditions for a genuine dialogue between the churches, drawing attention both to the welcome emphasis in Roman Catholic writing on the 'ecclesial community of baptized Christians' and also to such things as the problems of religious liberty and the difficulties caused by the present Roman canon law on mixed marriages.

The third event was the entry at New Delhi as members of the World Council of Churches of the Orthodox Churches of Russia, Bulgaria, Rumania and Poland, 'at the very moment when Orthodoxy has given a fresh sign of its unity after the Rhodes Conference'. We could look forward to a life-giving enrichment of our dialogue from this increased Orthodox participation, particularly perhaps from the Orthodox doctrine of the Holy Spirit and the Orthodox conception of tradition. 'All these reasons give us cause to rejoice that the Orthodox Churches now occupy a stronger position within the World Council.'

The fourth event was the series of negotiations for union between member-churches of the World Council, some of them between churches in different confessional traditions. How was all this to be interpreted, especially since the movement towards unity was strongest where churches knew they were in a missionary situation? It was a sign of the way in which the times called to the Church for both unity and mission. 'As soon as circumstances make the urgency of the missionary task more apparent, the churches realize the equally urgent need for unity.'

These union schemes and the unions themselves were not, of course, permanent resting places. This was made clear by our differences about intercommunion and about the relation of intercommunion to complete visible unity. Moreover, the churches did not exist for themselves but for the world. What was the meaning for the Church of the presence today of a single technological civilization throughout the world? What (to put it another way) was the relation between the *world-wide* and the *ecumenical*? In our concern for the unity of the Church we were confronted with a single problem: the rediscovery that either we should together attain to the universality that is centred in Christ the Lord of history, or we should not attain to it at all.

After Commissioner Booth of the Salvation Army, President of the Canadian Council of Churches, had welcomed the Conference to the Dominion of Canada, Dr Albert C. Outler (Methodist Church, U.S.A.), in a paper entitled 'From Disputation to Dialogue',[1] dwelt on the meta-

---

[1] For the full text of this address, see *The Ecumenical Review*, October 1963, pp. 14-23.

morphosis in the texture and quality of relations between divided Christians that had taken place in the past half-century. He described this as the shift from polemical disputation to ecumenical dialogue, and went on to detect the sources of this new attitude not only in the life of the churches but also in the Renaissance dialogue form characterized by the *aim* of persuasion and the *method* of accurate statement of opposed views.

'The Conference itself', he said, 'will be an experiment in dialogue; what it does and says and the plans it makes will go far to decide whether the enterprise of doctrinal dialogue can be spread throughout the churches and become a dynamic influence in their renewal.' The Faith and Order Movement might now be most needed to help the generality of churchmen to be drawn out of relative isolation into conference with their fellow Christians. If this was going to be possible, we must ourselves be truly committed to the way of dialogue.

This 'way of dialogue' required four things: *the disposition to listen creatively*, so that one heard what the other man intended to say rather than merely what his words could be made to mean; *the disposition to be affected* by what one heard, recognizing that such changes in oneself were often both slow and indirect; the *willingness to speak up*, as clearly, as graciously and as explicitly as possible; and the *acceptance of responsibility to keep the dialogue moving*, in the faith that if when deadlocks occurred they were lived with intelligently, they would in due season be transcended.

Ecumenical dialogue was not, of course, open at both its ends. It could only proceed within the community of faith in Jesus Christ, and it depended upon our mutual recognition of each other as fellow members of that community. It also depended upon our marking carefully the difference between the mystery of God's self-revelation and the validity of any form of human speech that acknowledged and interpreted this mystery; 'the faith once delivered to the saints' was not delivered to them on a parchment of propositions. Thirdly, the dialogue depended on the recognition that the sovereign cure for ignorance and error was neither disputation nor mere toleration, but love. 'Dialogue must be intent upon the truth, or else be a deception; it must proceed in love, or else it will never come to the whole truth.'

Formal Actions of the Conference   The business session that followed, presided over by Dr Douglas Horton, Chairman of the Commission on Faith and Order, adopted the rules of the Conference and elected amidst applause Dr Oliver S. Tomkins, Bishop of Bristol (Church of England), as chairman of the Conference, and the Most Rev. Chrysostomos, Metropolitan of Myra, Professor Henri D'Espine, and Professor Albert C. Outler, as vice-chairmen. It agreed with acclamation to send affectionate greetings from the Conference to Dr Leonard Hodgson, to M. Marc Boegner, and to Bishop Otto Dibelius, three leaders to whom Faith and Order owed much.

The Task of the Montreal Conference In General Session, the Bishop of Bristol gave the third of the introductory addresses, dealing with the scope of the Conference against the background of Dr Mehl's delineation of the point we had reached in the ecumenical pilgrimage, and Dr Outler's analysis of the essential methods of dialogue.

The Conference, he said, would build upon foundations laid in the past: upon the accumulated work of the Faith and Order Movement and of the World Council of Churches, including the New Delhi Statement. More particularly, it had before it the four reports of its Theological Commissions on 'Christ and the Church', on 'Tradition and Traditions', on 'Worship', and on 'Institutionalism'. (These have been published in one volume as *Faith and Order Findings*, SCM Press and Augsburg Publishing House, 1963.)

After reviewing briefly the reports of these Commissions, Dr Tomkins went on to ask some questions about the work of Faith and Order. First, about method: in an age when the churches were in conference in many diverse ways, would the short-term working party on a specific subject serve our aims better than the longer-term and more general committee? Would it more easily justify asking busy men to take part? Could there be a more careful use of regional resources which would yet avoid the dangers of undue provincialism? Secondly, what was the place of Faith and Order in the W.C.C. as a whole? Here the essential requirements were two. Within the whole W.C.C. staff there should be a staff adequate to undertake the Faith and Order work that the member churches want done; and representatives of the Faith and Order Commission and its staff must be properly heard when the major policy of the W.C.C. as a whole was decided.

A third group of questions concerned the work itself: 'Are we in danger of a theological provincialism in which certain theological trends (for example the Bultmannian) are not adequately reflected in our work? Ought we not to take a more responsible interest in the many movements towards actual organic union? Above all else, is our awareness that of a decisive moment, a *kairos* of unity? At the Lund Conference we said that the very gifts which God has given to us in the unity movement will become a judgement on us instead of a blessing if we are not ready to follow out the implications of what we have already received. We are today ever more aware of the implications of unity for missions, for truth, for holiness. 'If we obey God costingly in his demand for unity, we shall thereby find that we are being brought face to face with his other demands. . . . Let us pray that by taking further steps in obedience to that Will, we shall find ourselves blessed in every area of our life.'

Section Meetings In the afternoon the five Sections had their first meeting. It is more convenient to describe their work section by section, and this is done on pp. 18–31.

The Holy Communion In the evening the Conference met for a service of preparation for Holy Communion, conducted in the Presbyterian Church of St Andrew and St Paul by Dr J. Robert Nelson, Professor in the Graduate School of Theology at Oberlin (Methodist Church, U.S.A.). The sermon, on I Tim. 3.16 ('For confessedly, great is the mystery of our religion: He who was manifested in the body . . .'), was preached by Professor J. K. S. Reid of Aberdeen University (Church of Scotland).

On Sunday morning, July 14th, the Conference was welcomed to a service of the Holy Communion in Erskine and American Church of the United Church of Canada. The minister, the Rev. Norman M. Slaughter, officiated, assisted by Dr George Johnston, Principal of the United Theological College, Montreal. The sermon, on Mark 1.15 'Repent and believe the Gospel', was preached by the Rev. Dr J. Russell Chandran, Principal of the United Theological College, Bangalore (Church of South India).

These opening activities of the first three days did in fact do what they had been planned to do. They placed the Conference in its setting in the common life of the churches as it is today, reminding us of our past inheritance and yet freeing us from bondage to it. The three 'key-note' addresses complemented one another, moving on a single line of thought from the position of fellowship into which the churches have now come to the quality of the conversation which that fellowship makes necessary, and concluding with some practical reflections on the work of the Conference in providing the material for that conversation.

In these opening sessions, also, some of the characteristic notes of the Conference were struck—Rome, the Orthodox, the Afro-Asians, and we became familiar both with the comfort of our accommodation and the discomfort of the heat and noise of the Winter Stadium.

Yet the opening actions were perhaps not wholly satisfactory. The 'key-note addresses' had a single line of thought—could they not, perhaps, have been compressed into one paper? And were the questions posed with sufficient clarity? One voices the doubt only in the wisdom or unwisdom of hindsight. But to the end, it seemed, the Conference remained a little uncertain of its precise object. There is an *embarras de richesses* in the way of proposals for further study in the Section

Reports which suggests that the Conference also remained uncertain to the end about the role of Faith and Order.

Perhaps these ambiguities were symbolized in the service of Holy Communion. The Eucharist provides in any case the strongest symbol both of our unity and disunity, and of our uncertainty about how best to affirm the one and diminish the other. But this particular service was symbolic in other ways also. For some—probably the majority—it was a deeply moving occasion. Others found themselves remaining relatively undisturbed. Others again—a minority, probably small and possibly very significant—were not so much unmoved as provoked by the service into demanding an altogether different kind of Christian worship.

But this is only to say that in its unity and its disunity, in its affirmations and in its doubts, Montreal was from beginning to end a true reflection of the churches whose creation it was.

II. WORSHIP AND BIBLE STUDY

On the mornings of July 15, 16, 17, 18, 19 and 24, morning prayers and Bible study took place in the sections under the following leaders:

Sections I—Dr G. R. Beasley-Murray (Baptist Union of Great Britain and Ireland)
II—Dr C. H. Hwang (Presbyterian Church in Formosa)
III—Dr Jean Bosc (Reformed Church of France)
IV—Dr J. A. Sittler (Lutheran Church in America)
V—Bishop F. Sigg (The Methodist Church, U.S.A.)

On the other mornings, prayers were led in plenary sessions by the following:

July 13—Metropolitan Athenagoras of Elaia (Greek Orthodox)
20—Professor Henri d'Espine (Swiss Protestant Church Federation)
22—Professor Joseph A. Johnson (Christian Methodist Episcopal Church, U.S.A.)
23—Professor H. Sawyerr (Church of the Province of West Africa)
25—Professor R. F. Aldwinckle (Baptist Federation of Canada)
26—Dr Maurice Creasey (London Yearly Meeting of the Society of Friends).

Evening prayers throughout the Conference were taken with the assistance of a booklet of intercession, *Let us Pray for Unity*, prepared for the Conference by Dr J. Robert Nelson (published by The Upper Room, Nashville, Tenn., U.S.A.).

There is no point at which the inherent difficulties of the world-wide ecumenical movement are felt more acutely than in worship, because there is no point at which one is usually more dependent upon the use of the language and the tradition to which one is accustomed. So difficult indeed is this cluster of problems that the technique of worship in ecumenical gatherings has not yet received the attention it deserves. It should be recorded therefore that the arrangements made at Montreal and the way in which they were carried out indicated that, if there is so much yet to be done in this delicate and complex field, some progress has nevertheless been made.

III. THE EVENING SESSIONS

On Monday, July 15, Dr Henri D'Espine presided over a General Session on 'Catholicity'. Dr Lukas Vischer, Research Secretary of the Faith and Order Department of the W.C.C. and moderator of the session, drew attention to the way in which the ecumenical movement had avoided the use of the term 'catholicity' because of its past polemical associations with the self-assertion of separated churches; but he insisted that we had now to listen to the word and the idea and explore it together.

Archpriest Vitaly Borovoy (Russian Orthodox Church), speaking in English, expounded the Orthodox Church's biblical and patristic understanding of the catholicity of the Church, 'which is not only her inalienable possession but also her basic task'. Professor Claude Welch (Methodist Church, U.S.A.) noted that though Protestantism had always affirmed its catholicity, it had not much explored its content. He proposed that we should think of it as a 'master image' that seized the mind of the Church in its self-understanding because it expressed vital dimensions of the Church's relation to God in Jesus Christ: it pointed to the wholeness of the truth in Jesus Christ; it ordered and identified the Church's mission; and it allowed us to be satisfied with nothing less than the most inclusive possible expression of the richness of Christ.[1]

Brief comments on the papers were made by Professor Dale Moody (Southern Baptist Convention) and Canon H. M. Waddams (Church of England).

On Tuesday, July 16, the Metropolitan of Myra presided over a session on 'The Church in the New Testament'. Professor Paul S. Minear, Director of the Faith and Order Department, and moderator of the session, described the sometimes embarrassing contacts of the ecumenical movement with the biblical historian and the biblical theologian, and introduced Professor Ernst Käsemann (Evangelical Church in Germany) and Professor Raymond E. Brown, S.S. (Roman Catholic Church, U.S.A.), who gave addresses on 'Unity and Diversity in New Testament Ecclesiology'.

[1] For the full text of Archpriest Borovoy's and Professor Welch's addresses, see *The Ecumenical Review*, October 1963, pp. 26-42.

Professor Käsemann reviewed the New Testament evidence and concluded: 'No romantic postulate, dressed up as *Heilsgeschichte*, can relativize the sober fact that the historian simply cannot speak of an unbroken unity of New Testament ecclesiology, for he perceives there the early pattern of our situation, with its differences, dilemmas and antitheses.' Yet early Christianity did proclaim the one Church. How did it do it, and how can we do it? 'My own conviction is that this problem cannot be approached on a purely historical level. The unity of the Church has been, is, and remains primarily an eschatological datum, which is only achieved in so far as it is received as a gift.'

Professor Brown, after noticing recent works on some critical questions regarding the Gospels, the Acts of the Apostles, and the Pastoral Epistles, concluded that we could speak of continuity in New Testament theology, but that we must do so in terms of 'the Spirit of Christ which constantly brought out the meaning of Jesus for the new circumstances in which his followers found themselves'. The picture was not simply one of progress in a straight line towards a uniform position; but there was a 'unity of belief present in all stages of New Testament thought about the Church'. This contention he illustrated by discussing the Church's catholicity with reference to the Gospel, to the Twelve and the apostles in general, and to the Sacraments of Baptism and the Eucharist.

Short comments on these positions were given by Professor J. Davis McCaughey (Presbyterian Church of Australia) and Professor G. W. H. Lampe (Church of England).

On Thursday, July 18, Dr Albert C. Outler presided over a session on the theme 'Faith and Order Today: Self-Examination and Prospect'. As moderator, the Rev. Patrick C. Rodger, Executive Secretary of the Faith and Order Department, recalled the Bishop of Bristol's fear of the danger of 'theological provincialism' and introduced an exploration of the relations of the Faith and Order Movement to those at present outside its membership.

First, Dr Hans Harms (Evangelical Church in Germany) reviewed the dialogue with the Church of Rome from the bleak beginnings of the interview of some of the founders of the movement with Pope Benedict XV in 1919 to the 'miracle of the Holy Spirit' in the brief pontificate of Pope John XXIII. Dr Harms asked however, rather sharply, whether there was a real chance for a real dialogue between equals, and what the Church of Rome really believed about the Holy Spirit.

Secondly, Dr Chow Lien-Hwa (Taiwan Baptist Convention) in a paper on 'Dialogue with Independent Evangelicals' discussed in vivid detail the fears and suspicions of many with whom he had close contact. They did not trust the theology of the member churches of the World Council. They considered that its all-inclusive programme took the

W.C.C. into social and political issues which were not its concern. They feared that it would develop into a World Church in which small groups would be dominated by large, their voice unheard and their God-given work jeopardized. From this Dr Chow went on to speak of the difficulty and the hope of ecumenical work among Evangelicals, where one must talk about similarities rather than about differences, emphasize major issues rather than minor ones, and start from faith rather than from dogma. Above all, he said, 'for us who are interested in the ecumenical dialogue, our Christian character is exceptionally important'.

The third speaker, Mr William Stringfellow (Protestant Episcopal Church, U.S.A.), in an address on 'The Freedom of God' asked very sharply indeed whether the Faith and Order Movement had grasped that 'the real issues of faith and order are simply the ordinary issues of life and death in the world. . . . Modern thinking and unthinking man does not care a hoot about the Faith and Order Movement, because Faith and Order apparently does not care about him.' The cure for this state of affairs was partly a reconstruction of the policy of Faith and Order such that ordinary parsons and ordinary workers could take part. But it was partly, and much more deeply, a reconstruction of the way we understand theology. This could be illustrated from the racial crisis in America 'which now has the stature of an insurrection', and about which the churches had failed to state the truth. 'By the word of God, the substantive issue in the racial crisis is baptism—not the survival of the American experiment, not democracy, not the vanities of humanism, but baptism. For baptism—this agenda item for Faith and Order—is the sacrament of the unity among men wrought by God in overcoming the power and reign of death. . . . Baptism—that Faith and Order issue—is the central issue in the racial crisis because baptism is the sacrament of the reconciliation of all men and all creation in the life of God. . . . Baptism is the secret by which a society is healed of racism.'

Dr E. A. Payne (Baptist Union of Great Britain and Ireland) and Dean K. V. Sarkissian (Armenian Apostolic Church, Catholicosate of Cilicia) made short comments on the theme of the evening.

IV. THE SECTIONS

The entire membership of the Conference (including advisers, observers and guests) was divided into five Sections:

  I. The Church in the Purpose of God
 II. Scripture, Tradition and Traditions
III. The Redemptive Work of Christ and the Ministry of the Church
 IV. Worship and the Oneness of Christ's Church
  V. 'All in Each Place': The Process of Growing Together

These Sections were each given the task of producing a 3,000-word report, for consideration in Plenary Sessions towards the end of the Conference, and were instructed that this Report should be written as far as possible in terms which ordinary educated Christians without theological training could understand. In order to make more detailed study possible, each Section was further divided for part of its work into three or four Sub-sections of about twenty people each.

The Sections had before them as a basis for their work material of several kinds. There were, first, official W.C.C. reports and documents such as the report of the four Theological Commissions, collected in *Faith and Order Findings*;[1] separate publications which had grown out of the work of these commissions—the report on Baptism appearing as part of *One Lord, One Baptism* (SCM Press, 1960), and the symposium *Institutionalism and Church Unity* (Association Press and SCM Press, 1963); and other W.C.C. documents, such as the well-known statement of the Central Committee at Toronto, 1950, on *The Church, the Churches, and the World Council of Churches*.

Secondly, there was available in printed or duplicated form additional material prepared by the W.C.C. staff, by National Councils of Churches, or by informal groups of Roman Catholic or independent Evangelical scholars. The principal documents available are listed in detail under each Section.

The Sections has at their disposal the resource—more valuable still—of the experience of the participants themselves. Since the Sub-sections were small enough to allow their members to understand and be understood, this resource could be put to work.

In formal Section or Sub-section meeting, as well as in the private conversation which is the intimate centre of any ecumenical gathering, each of us was made vividly aware of the background of this or that participant, and in that awareness entered into something of the grandeur and misery, the mystery and hope, of the position of the whole Church in the whole world. A Section discussing the secularization of the world could not fail to discern a wealth of meaning in the cheerful assurance of a delegate from the U.S.S.R.: 'We are the *experts* on secularization.' A Section discussing local disunity would listen to the bewilderment of a West African, expressed with a taut restraint that emphasized his depth of feeling, that Christian people could practise a colour-bar actually inside the Church. Moments of this kind were many. So also were those which brought a group sharply up against the realities of church life, in which our divided state may still prevent ecumenical action and impose a hard choice between inaction on the one hand and competing denominational actions on the other.

The Montreal Conference marked a new stage of the participation of

[1] See p. 13 above.

Orthodox delegates and Roman Catholic observers. There has probably
been no major W.C.C. conference in which the Orthodox Churches
have been so fully immersed or have taken so active a part at every
stage. (This full participation was much assisted by a consultation of
Orthodox and non-Orthodox theologians held immediately before the
Conference opened.) This has created a new situation, both for them
and for the Western churches whose ways of work and thought had
previously shaped the ecumenical movement. The Orthodox formerly
seemed content to allow discussions to go on in whatever way the majority
wanted, reserving to themselves the right to make a dissenting statement at the end. They now insisted on playing as decisive a role as
anyone else in the shaping of the discussions and the structure and
contents of the report to be produced. For some people, both in the
East and the West, the tensions that sometimes resulted were frustrating.
For others, again on both sides, they were to be welcomed as a challenge
to a richer and deeper dialogue than we have yet experienced as Churches.

At New Delhi, the Roman Catholic observers had behaved 'cor-
rectly' in the sense that, though they had taken part with enthusiasm,
with one exception they had not spoken in formal meeting. It is a mark
of the progress that had taken place in the nineteen months between
New Delhi and Montreal, that in Montreal a main paper in General
Session was given by a Roman Catholic scholar, and that in Section
and Sub-section it was usually impossible to tell the status of the participants, since all participated with equal freedom.

There was a dramatic moment in one Sub-section, when two distinguished ecumenical theologians, one Presbyterian and the other Roman
Catholic, agreed on the proposition: 'When *you* celebrate the Eucharist,
our Lord is present, and *I* am present with Him.' It is also true that a
later attempt by an Anglican and others to get this specific point
included in the report was unacceptable to some Reformed, Lutheran
and Orthodox opinion, and had to be abandoned.

Such stories could be multiplied, but they must not be misunderstood.
If some issues notoriously cut across confessional lines, others as
notoriously do not. If there is an astonishing renewal in Rome and an
astonishing possibility of fellowship, the hard facts to which Dr Harms
and Dr Mehl alluded still remain. There is also Dr Karl Barth's
warning that we shall do best to concentrate not on the new relations
now possible with Rome but on what is happening in and to Rome
herself, and to ask whether we are ourselves similarly open to the word
of the Spirit.[1]

---

[1] This may be the place to remark that the well-provided conference book-
stall, run by the staff of the SCM Book Room, Toronto, reported the following
as its best-sellers: *Honest to God* by Dr John A. T. Robinson, Bishop of Wool-
wich; two paper-back introductions to the life of the Orthodox Church; and
Xavier Rynne's *Letters from Vatican City*.

SECTION 1: *The Church in the Purpose of God*

The basic document before Section I was the report of the Theological Commission on 'Christ and the Church' which contains the two quite distinct reports of the North American and European Sections of the Commission. *Faith and Order Findings* in which they are reprinted includes neither contents page nor index; it seems desirable therefore to say that the North American report will be found on page 9 of that book's second report and the European on page 37.

The Section also had at its disposal the report of the three other Theological Commissions and (like the other four Sections) a study guide, prepared by a drafting group which met at Bossey a month before the Conference began. In addition there was made available from all over the world a wealth of comment on 'Christ and the Church' —from Nashville, Tennessee, from five Roman Catholic scholars in the British Isles, from Fr Jan Groot of the Netherlands, and from a group of Conservative Evangelical scholars in North America. From South and Central Africa came papers on independent or separatist church movements and their relation to the Church and the churches. On the subject of the meaning of Councils of Churches, there was 'the Toronto Statement',[1] a paper by Archbishop Iakovos (Greek Orthodox Church, U.S.A.), the Report on 'The Ecclesiological Significance of Councils of Churches' of the National Council of Churches in the U.S.A., and an essay by the Rev. Kenneth Slack of the British Council of Churches. There was also a staff paper summarizing what the official documents of the W.C.C. had said about the meaning of membership in that body.[2] There was, finally, a paper of excerpts from an article by R. S. French, 'Holy Communion in Ecumenical Gatherings', originally published in the Youth Department *Bulletin*, No. 6, December 1962.

This mass of material was, perhaps, somewhat daunting to the neophyte (the old Faith and Order hand would have seen some of it before and would anyhow have worked out a technique for handling it economically or even not handling it at all). But if it was read, and by most people it was, it would go a long way to ensure that the discussion was really broadly based.

When discussion in the Section began, it fastened on the report on *Christ and the Church* of which (especially of the European portion) the Section was exceedingly critical. It may be noted, incidentally, that the North American group of Conservative Evangelicals was more critical of the North American report, and more in sympathy with the

[1] See p. 19 above.
[2] Cp. W. A. Visser 't Hooft, 'The Meaning of Membership', *Minutes of the Central Committee of the W.C.C., Rochester, 1963*, pp. 134-8.

European. The core of this criticism of the European report was that its theology made a connection between Christ and the Church, and between the disciples and the apostles, which was more direct than the New Testament evidence allowed. It was stressed that the link from Christ to the Church is one that passes through the radical break of Christ's death and resurrection. Further, some members of the Section were critical of the tendency in the report (and elsewhere) to speak too much of the impersonal 'mighty acts of God' and too little of the person of Christ himself. In this discussion, the Section reflected the contemporary critical attitude to certain aspects of biblical theology. Perhaps, as Dr Paul Minear had pointed out, 'biblical theology' has been more easily accepted in the ecumenical movement than the actual findings of biblical scholars. This was one of the points where positions taken in a General Session—in this case particularly that of Prof. Ernst Käsemann—had a direct bearing on the work of the Sections.[1]

The Section divided into four Sub-sections:

(i) Christ, New Creation, Creation
(ii) The Church: Act and Institution
(iii) Christ, The Church and the Churches
(iv) The Church and the World Council of Churches

The first draft of the Section report came before a full session of the Conference on July 22nd, at the end of a hot, hurried, and weary day wholly spent in the Winter Stadium which, however admirable it may be for ice-hockey, is acoustically little suited for discussion and is aesthetically repellent for worship. (This sour comment may, I hope, be excused if I add to it a grateful word for the unalloyed excellence of all the other arrangements.) In these circumstances, the Conference in deliberative sessions was not able to give the best of its mind to the Report.

Professor G. R. Cragg on introducing it admitted candidly the divergences of opinion in the Section, spoke of the intensity of controversy, mitigated by charity and good humour, that had characterized the discussion, and drew attention to the fact that it would be found in the Report that 'often behind a seemingly innocuous sentence there lies a delicate balance, very patiently achieved'.

In plenary discussion, Professor Dinkler and others returned once more to the question of the different ways in which the Church is understood in the New Testament. How, he asked, had the plurality of the New Testament ecclesiologies been overcome in the Report? The answer: By insisting, as the Report did, on the indivisibility of the crucifixion and the resurrection. The Church was the body of the

---

[1] These considerations illustrate the importance of a consultation of New Testament scholars held in Montreal immediately after the Conference ended, and attended by some who had been present at it, and others who had not.

crucified and risen Lord; and it was therefore the suffering Church which was the blessed Church. But this understanding was not consistently carried through, said these critics, and there were traces elsewhere of a different theology—that of an *ecclesia triumphans*.

The idea of Christ as the Servant, 'the man for others', is an idea of power in our time; and the idea of the Church as *servant* inspires especially those reformers who are most critical of the remaining traces of the 'Constantinian' epoch. Yet we may be sure that there will not be unanimous support in the churches for a consistent re-interpretation along these lines of our doctrine of the Church and its place in society.

There was, moreover, profound disagreement about the ecclesiological significance of the World Council itself. Outside the ecumenical movement there are many who accuse the World Council of being, or wishing to become, a super-church. Within it, there are those (especially, most Orthodox) who are unwilling to attach to it much theological significance; and others who find themselves compelled by their experience together in the World Council to affirm that they find in it at least some 'churchly' qualities. What the Conference was able finally to agree to say will be found in the Report on page 48, which can be profitably compared with the Toronto statement on *The Church, the Churches, and the World Council of Churches*. This debate will certainly go on.

SECTION II: *Scripture, Tradition and Traditions*

The Section had before it the report of the Commission on 'Tradition and Traditions' (*Faith and Order Findings*, fourth report), the earlier publication called *The Old and the New in The Church* (SCM Press, 1961), and a staff working paper. It also had a series of essays from Prof. J. L. Leuba, Dr E. Flesseman van Leer, Prof. S. L. Greenslade, Prof. K. Bonis, and Prof. G. Ebeling of the European Section of the Commission;[1] a paper giving extracts from regional studies in Kyoto, Tokyo, Bombay, France and North America; a comment on the Commission Report by Père Yves Congar, O.P.; two staff papers, one raising questions about the Councils of the Early Church in their bearing on the ecumenical movement, and the other on the Catechisms of member churches; a paper on traditions and the Christian mission; and a paper on the formation of a Japanese Protestant tradition. The amount of the evidence for the 'younger churches' in this list is impressive, and very necessary. For it is in the planting and nurturing of new churches that the question 'What are we spreading: our denomination or the Catholic Church?' becomes most inescapable; and it is today pressed upon us with increasing passion by Asians and Africans, as the report of the All-Africa Conference of Churches at Kampala

[1] Later published as *Schrift und Tradition*, EVZ-Verlag, Zurich.

(April 1963) attests. But it is likely also that the lessons learned in the old 'mission field' will be directly valuable in the new 'mission field' of urban civilization and of technological culture.

The working paper presented to this group proposed a definition of Tradition (derived in part from the Commission Report) substantially wider than has been customary: 'Tradition in all its aspects, viewed in a Trinitarian perspective, is understood as the total process in which God the Son and God the Holy Spirit, sent by the Father, enter time and history and submit to their conditions in order to bring about their subjection to a fulfilment in Christ.' The discussion in the Section fastened on this definition, and, as the report of the Section shows, generally accepted it. The point is far from merely academic, as will become clear once the question is discussed in the churches. There are churches 'whose tradition it is to pay little regard to tradition'; there are churches which appear to exalt one tradition of interpretation of the Bible, a tradition which may be completely taken for granted. The new terminology is proposed in an attempt to by-pass the old road-blocks, and also to elucidate the traditional positions. It deserves to be considered with care.

The Section divided into the following three Sub-sections:

(i) The Role of Scripture in the Traditionary Process
(ii) The Unity of the Tradition and the Diversity of Traditions
(iii) The Christian Tradition and Cultural Diversity.

When the first drafts of the Section reports were presented to the whole conference on July 22nd, Section II was only in a position to present a draft from its first Sub-section. This showed that the Section had accepted the 'new understanding' of Tradition and thought of 'the Tradition' as the Gospel itself, Christ himself present in the life of the Church. 'The Tradition' thus understood came to us in tradition, in the sense of the traditionary process. Our traditions are of three kinds —our diverse traditions of forms of expression; our diverse confessional traditions; and our diverse cultural traditions. But the Section went further, and proposed a paragraph as follows:

'In our present situation, we wish to consider the problem of Scripture and Tradition, or rather that of Tradition and Scripture. Our starting-point is that we are all living in a tradition which goes back to our Lord and has its roots in the Old Testament, and we are all indebted to that tradition, inasmuch as we have received the revealed truth, the Gospel, through its being transmitted from one generation to another. Thus we can say that we exist as Christians *sola traditione*, by tradition alone. Tradition then in this sense includes the preaching of the Word and worship, Christian teaching and theology, missions, and also witness to Christ in the lives of members of the Church.'

Both Frère Max Thurian of Taizé and Professor Ernst Käsemann of Tübingen, from their different points of view, said that although they accepted the term *sola traditione* in this context, they thought it would certainly be impossible to maintain it for wider use; it would unquestionably cause serious misunderstanding, especially among Protestants already suspicious of the W.C.C. and accustomed to *sola Scriptura* as the battle-cry of the Reformation. (Echoes of the speeches in General Session by Dr Hans Harms and Dr Chow Lien-Hwa could perhaps be heard here.) Nevertheless, the phrase is perhaps difficult only because it is premature; and it is likely, when used as a summary of a whole understanding of Tradition in this sense, to be of real value in ecumenical work. Such a use of it will, however, also need to take into account the warning notes sounded in the discussion on behalf of Scripture, if not of *sola Scriptura*. In particular, it was asked, where is this Tradition to be authoritatively found? Ought not more to be said about the significance of the Canon of Scripture?

The final version of the Report abandoned the dangerous phrase; but it will probably live on, not less powerful for being unofficial. The whole approach, indeed, of this Section is full of promise for divided Churches struggling to discover their unity. Once it has been translated into terms the churches at large can make use of, it will be as welcome as rivers of water in a dry land.

SECTION III: *The Redemptive Work of Christ and the Ministry of the Church*

No theological commission on the ministry was appointed at Lund and there was therefore no Commission Report specifically addressed to the Section. Parts of the Report on 'Christ and the Church' were of course relevant, and were reprinted in *Laity Bulletin* No. 15 (May 1963) of the Laity Department of the W.C.C. This also included a long and important paper prepared by that Department on 'Christ's Ministry through his whole Church and its Ministers'.

Presented to members of the Section, in addition, were a paper of the Division of World Mission and Evangelism entitled 'A Tent-Making Ministry',[1] on the question of a ministry both non-professional and non-stipendiary; a paper by Dr Edmund Schlink on the Apostolic Succession;[2] some extracts from regional studies in Japan, India, and North America; a series of eight papers on the ordination of women by Reformed, Anglican, and Orthodox theologians (the W.C.C.'s Department on Cooperation of Men and Women had assisted Faith

[1] Available from Publications Department W.C.C.
[2] German original published in *Kerygma und Dogma*, 7/2 (1961), pp. 79-114; English translation in *Encounter*, Indianapolis, 1964.

and Order in the preparation of these);[1] Fr Jan Groot's criticisms of the
Report on 'Christ and the Church'; and a paper by Dr Lukas Vischer
on the diaconate.

The question of the ministry has not been prominent in Faith and
Order discussions for some twenty-five years. In those years there
has, of course, been a continuing spate of books about the ministry,
many of them of the kind which attempts the constructive re-statement
of the doctrine of a particular church or confessional tradition in the
light of criticism from other traditions. This type of work can be
a valuable, indeed essential, element in the whole ecumenical conversation. But it is probably true to say that two other things have
exercised a far greater and fresher influence on thinking about the
ministry in those twenty-five years. One of these is the recovery of a
doctrine of the whole Church as the people of God, and of a positive
and indeed creative understanding of the laity in consequence. The
other is the accompanying recovery of the sense that the Church, the
ministry, and the congregation are all alike in basic principle missionary,
though much of the structure we have inherited from the past makes it
difficult to practise this principle and to act upon it.

In the absence of a Report from a Theological Commission, the staff
working-paper was necessarily of particular importance to the Section.
But the latter had some difficulty in accepting this paper as determining
the line of its work. One reason for this was that in some churches
there is a profound uneasiness about the 'new line' about the laity (the
Laity Department even being stigmatized as a sacred cow, inaccessible
to criticism), while in others the 'new line' has been so influential that
there is a considerable reluctance, even among the ordained, to say
anything very positive at all about the ordained ministry. In ecumenical discussions the ministry is usually characterized as 'special' or
'set apart' in order to avoid identifying it exclusively either with any
particular theology of orders, or with the professional full-time and
stipendiary ministry. Both on the theology and on the voluntary/
professional issue there has been much fresh thinking. This last concern
has been much stimulated by studies in the Division of World Mission
and Evangelism, and experiments both in the younger churches and
in the de-christianized cities of the West.

The Section had therefore a very difficult task; and it is not entirely
surprising that Professor J. D. McCaughey, Chairman of the Section,
in introducing this draft to the whole Conference, should have confessed that not much headway had been made. The main body of the
Report was presented as a series of theses on the ministry formulated
in the attempt to penetrate 'behind our divisions to a deeper and richer
understanding of the mystery of the God-given unity of Christ with

---

[1] See *Concerning the Ordination of Women*, W.C.C., 1964.

his Church' (Lund Report). The discussion in deliberative session largely consisted in detailed criticism of these theses, though one striking exception was a passionate demand from a Nigerian for more emphasis on what the whole Conference could *agree* to say together: 'We are being bullied by the older churches. Vague statements are of no use to us in our church unity negotiations.'

In introducing the final Report, Professor McCaughey referred to the notorious difficulty of speaking briefly, clearly, and unitedly about the apostolate, the ministry which was both something given to the apostles and also part of the content of their preaching. Moreover, there were the well-known historical problems. But the Section believed that Dr Edmund Schlink's paper on the Apostolic Succession which had been before them might prove to be the starting-point for a new discussion which must indeed be both systematically and dogmatically theological, but need not break down into mere interconfessional controversy. The Section of the Report on the threefold office of Christ (paragraph 89) had been substantially rewritten in response to the criticism made at the deliberative session and the subsequent hearing. The discussion prompted in his mind a question: why are Protestants so anxious to secure the unique unrepeatable once-for-all character of the work of Christ as *Priest*, and so little concerned to do the same for his work as *Prophet* and *King*? Dr McCaughey also drew attention to the importance of the discussion on the special ministry, which Faith and Order could no longer ignore. Many member churches were involved in actual union negotiations and Faith and Order should be in a position to help them as they might request. But we must also reckon with a widespread loss of nerve about the ministry. We needed to work together at a doctrine of the ministry which was less a matter of controversy and more a stimulus to obedience. The four appendices to the Report made proposals for further work to the Faith and Order Commission.

In plenary discussion there was a spirited attack by Professor D. W. Hay (Presbyterian Church in Canada) on the way in which the idea of the *Shepherd* has disappeared from the report's account of the office of Christ and also of the work of the special ministry. The proposal in Appendix I was worded in a way which prejudiced the study in favour of the Laity Department's understanding of the ministry as concerned almost exclusively with building up the laity for ministry and mission, and against the traditional understanding (which was what ordinary people looked for in the clergy). Moreover, this 'new' doctrine needed to be much more securely grounded in scientific exegesis of the New Testament.

It may not be irrelevant to observe that this 'parson *versus* people' discussion would be illustrated by a study of the ways in which parson and people act in practice as pastors and shepherds to *each other*. The problem is made a little more difficult for Faith and Order in that this mutual shepherding is most easily experienced and practised in the parish rather than in the lecture room or the office.

The ordained ministry is the place where the churches feel their problems most acutely. Notoriously, it is the most difficult hurdle in many re-union negotiations; and we are now becoming uneasily aware that the difficulties of our stance in relation to the world are reflected in many countries and traditions in the unwillingness of young men to enter the pastoral ministry and the uncertainties of many in it. In these circumstances, the task in front of the Section necessarily appeared daunting, and its achievement very moderate. But if the Commission can discern the right way to follow up the new discussion Montreal has started, we may all yet be grateful to the Section for its labours.

SECTION IV: *Worship and the Oneness of Christ's Church*

This Section had before it the Report of the Theological Commission on 'Worship', which had worked in three sections: European, Asian, American (*Faith and Order Findings*, Part III, pp. 7, 29, 49, respectively). In addition to the staff working-paper and the report on Baptism,[1] it had a wealth of other material for reference. This included an essay on Intercommunion by Frère Max Thurian; the W.C.C. Youth Department's *Bulletin*, No. 6 (Dec. 1962), *Many Churches One Table One Church*; regional studies from Tokyo, Kyoto and California; papers on aspects of worship by J. C. Rylaarsdam and R. E. Cushman; Roman Catholic reactions from scholars in Holland, France, U.S.A. and Britain; the *Arnoldshain Theses* of 1958, a Lutheran-Reformed consensus on the Eucharist; papers on the Liturgical Movement by A. F. N. Lekkerkerker and Max Thurian; and a paper by R. E. Cushman on the predicament of Christian worship in the world today.

The Section was asked to deal with the request from the New Delhi Assembly that Faith and Order again consider the question of the Holy Communion at ecumenical gatherings, and see whether some revision of the Lund recommendations on that subject might be produced.

There were three Sub-sections:

(i) Worship and Man Today
(ii) Contemporary Issues in the Theology of Baptism and the Eucharist
(iii) Full Communion, Open Communion and Intercommunion.

The report of the third Sub-section on 'Communion Services at Ecumenical Gatherings' was not presented at a Deliberative Session (on July 22nd) but at a later Business Session (see p. 34 below). In the Report proper a modest advance was felt to have been achieved

---

[1] See p. 19 above.

in the passage on Sacrifice in the Eucharist since this is a subject traditionally regarded as altogether too difficult for any hope of a consensus. In plenary discussion attention was drawn to the insufficient emphasis on the eschatological note which is strongly marked, if not predominant, in all four accounts of the institution of the Eucharist in the New Testament.

Probably, however, the most significant thing about a report which was generally felt to be a good one was the main point made by the Section Chairman, President J. I. McCord (United Presbyterian Church, U.S.A.), in his introduction. The report, he said, represented the interaction of the Liturgical Revival with the ecumenical movement. The former had already been a very marked source of creative renewal in some churches (not least the present writer's Church of England), and continues to grow in others. It had not previously been fully recognized at a major W.C.C. gathering, and this is one more sign of the change in the climate since Lund. (One must add that the ecumenical movement has been a little slow about this. Fr Gabriel Hebert, S.S.M., who was a delegate at Lund, and died at Kelham during the Montreal Conference, published *Liturgy and Society*, that classic textbook of the Liturgical Movement, as long ago as 1935. And our understanding is as yet far from complete.) It was pointed out in discussion that (as might be expected in a document drawn up by theologians) the draft report made much mention of the word, but little of time and place. Sunday and the church year were neglected, and nothing at all had been said about the new church architecture— a contemporary movement of ecumenical cooperation between clergy and architects of different confessions.

The Section made some attempt to tackle questions of the indigenization of worship in Asia and Africa, but in the draft this treatment was felt to be far from satisfactory; and it was not clear to Africans whether the Section grasped for example the importance of *African* initiative in the preparation of a liturgy for Africa.

When the Report came back to the plenary session on July 25th, it did so substantially unchanged, but with two appendices containing recommendations, which were introduced by Principal Raymond George (Methodist Church, Great Britain), for two studies, on the nature of Christian worship and on the Sacraments of Baptism and the Eucharist.

In the plenary discussion, Principal G. R. Beasley-Murray (Baptist Union of Gt Britain and Ireland) expressed the hope that those who practised infant baptism and those who practised only believers' baptism would look, in their common study, at practice as well as at theology—e.g. at so-called 'indiscriminate baptism'. The Section agreed that the issues here might have been somewhat confused by the use of the phrase 'The unity of baptism' in the report *One Lord, One Baptism*.

If Section III seemed to be groping desperately and not too success-fully for new ways of tackling intractable difficulties, Section IV had the flavour of a party of pioneers who come suddenly in sight of a rich new land calling out for exploration.

SECTION V: *'All in Each Place': the Process of Growing Together*

The basic texts from which Section V started were the New Delhi Report on Unity, and especially the famous statement on the nature of the unity we seek, with the commentary upon it and its implications for local church life (*New Delhi Speaks*, SCM Press, 1962, pp. 55 ff.); and the Report of the Study Commission on 'Institutionalism' (*Faith and Order Findings*, first report). It also had, in addition to its staff working-paper, regional studies from Chile, Tokyo, Bombay and Bangalore, and the report of the three Asian 'Situation Conferences' held in 1963, on Joint Action for Mission; a paper on mission and unity from the W.C.C.'s Department of Studies in Evangelism; a paper by Daisuke Kitagawa (reprinted from the *Ecumenical Review*, October 1962) on racial and cultural issues in local unity; Roman Catholic comments on the Report on 'Institutionalism' from Fr B. Leeming, S.J., and Fr C. J. Dumont, O.P.; a paper by Bishop Emilianos Timiadis on ecumenical growth at the parish level; a short paper, stimulated by Asian churchmen, about the apostolate of local churches; and a paper by Dr Roy G. Ross, formerly of the National Council of Churches of Christ in U.S.A., on the 'Ecumenical Movement and the Local Church'.

This Section was clear that its duty was to try to speak intelligibly to the local church about its own responsibility. But it found considerable difficulty in keeping to its appointed field and not straying over into territory assigned to other Sections; and still further difficulties in arriving at an agreed definition of the meaning of the phrase 'local church', and at an agreed theology of the local church's relation to the whole Church (the *Una Sancta*). Part of this difficulty arose from a failure, experienced in other Sections as well, to arrive at a just estimate of the denominations and confessions which in practice (if not in the New Testament) are the link between the whole Church and the local church. In these matters there is a wide variety of easily hurt suscepti-bilities, not to speak of theological differences which are not easy to reconcile.

There were three Sub-sections:

(i) The Local Church and The Church Universal
(ii) The Church's Involvement in a Divided Society
(iii) The Mission of the People of God in Each Place

Local particularity—the peculiar character of the people and the place
—is the essence of the local church; and it does not lend itself to the
generalization necessary in a fairly brief report to a world gathering.
In the plenary Session, Section V's draft commanded an unenthusiastic
assent, tempered with the criticism from one Orthodox speaker that
the Report's understanding of the 'local church' was dubious, and
from some others that the report's strictures on the denominations were
not sufficiently severe.

In introducing the final Report, Dean Walter G. Muelder reminded
the Conference that this Section had addressed itself more specifically
to the local church, and had tried to make a serious attempt to investigate
the meaning of the phrase in the New Delhi Statement 'in each place'.
The recommendations had been carefully prepared by a special group
within the Section.

The Conference had been throughout uneasy about the relations and
the Church's part in the racial crisis. This feeling had been expressed
in the General Sessions by Mr William Stringfellow; it had come out
in a rather unsatisfactory informal meeting at which Dr Eugene
Carson Blake and others had explained the actions of the United
States' National Council of Christian Churches in the existing state
of racial crisis in that country. In the discussion of the Report of Section
V it was evident once again, both in the passionate insistence of a
Negro delegate that negroes were under-represented, and in the comment that the Section's recommendation on this subject was wrongly
phrased. What was wanted was not so much an evaluation of what the
churches already taught as new and clear teaching about the implications of Christian unity for membership of local churches.

The phrase 'non-theological factors' was much in the air in Section
V. There were those in its membership who insisted that it was theo-
logically false to call social, psychological and environmental considerations 'non-theological'. To do this seems to imply that men and women
are disembodied intelligences and that matter is outside the concern of
theology because outside the operations of God's care.

Let the sociologist and the psychologist and the practitioners of the
social and behavioural sciences therefore sit in with the theologian, the
philosopher and the church historian: this is the plea of Section V. In
return, other Sections might plead for a sustained attempt—especially
by the sociologists—to express the new critique in clear English. (If we
cannot write like Winston Churchill or Abraham Lincoln, at least let
Time magazine be a sort of example: it is a master of the exposition of
technical matter to lay audiences.) There is a 'non-theological' issue
here. Most theologians are brought up in a literary tradition which
makes them dislike the muddy turgidity too often affected by the
social scientists. So they miss the much needed message.

The Sections as a Whole

Finally, perhaps an attempt should be made to assess as a whole the process of work in the Sections—work which absorbed about two-thirds of the entire time and energy of the members of the Conference. There is an ebb and flow in work of this kind. The Conference began on a Friday. By the Monday, the Sections were wandering rather helplessly, uncertain whether the multitude of ideas would amount to more than flotsam and jetsam. By Wednesday morning it seemed that everyone to whom one spoke felt that a tide had come in and given the Sub-section at least one strong, clear thing to say. Two days later, Sub-sections reported to Sections, and saw their work dismissed by unsympathetic colleagues who knew nothing of the agonies and triumphs that had gone into those few tentative, almost precious pages; drafting committees were dotted about in every corner, and confidence had ebbed. By Tuesday, July 23rd, the hearings were over, the shape of the Reports was more or less fixed, and a sober confidence prevailed. Then remained the final day's polishing (or it might be a feverish attempt to secure agreement and to find a constructive way around an apparent impasse). After that, there were the final Plenary Sessions—and the judgement of our churches.

With this ebb and flow of hope and despondency was associated a fluctuation in the way members of the Conference estimated the whole process. Are these Reports, on which we labour so painfully, worthwhile? Does anybody read them, or are they the rubbish that some ecclesiastical top persons are reputed to consider them? And if they are not rubbish, is there not some way in which the process of composition could be reformed so as to allow, if not of elegance, at least of lucidity? And if they are certainly not lucid, and possibly not interesting or valuable, would we not be better employed in the agreeable processes of personal discussion and fellowship?

In opening the deliberative session on July 22nd, the Bishop of Bristol spoke of these doubts, and reminded us that we were expected, after all, to render some account of our stewardship to the churches which had appointed us and paid for us. The intensive work would be in the Sub-section and the Sections, where thorough discussion was possible, and something worth saying might be discovered. But that something needs to be widely representative, both of those who shared in its discovery and also of those who did not; and it also needs to be intelligible to these last. The process of submitting the intensive work of Sub-section and Section to the general scrutiny of the Conference as a whole is intended to help the delegates to discharge part of their duty —properly understood, a pastoral duty—to the churches. Nor is this all. It can be further argued that the tedious, sometimes infuriating, business of hammering out an agreed statement is a necessary discipline for divided sinners in search of unity. Without the discipline of the deadline for the Report should we struggle so hard to find something on which we *do* agree?

Yet questions remain. The process works triumphantly when there really *is* a consensus that is more comprehensive and deeper than had been believed before; and the churches will sense this, rise to it and make use of it. The New Delhi Statement (a revised version of something Faith and Order had originally given to the Central Committee at St Andrews in 1960) is a recent case in point. But what about those more numerous cases where the consensus is slighter, or can only be expressed in gobbledygook? Are the Reports then worth while?

We do not live in a static world; and one sign of this is that where once the ecumenical movement had a virtual monopoly of ecumenical literature, now the booksellers' shelves groan under the weight of the stuff, and no respectable 'religious' publisher is without his recent symposium on the state of the unity movement. Another factor is the occasional searing review of some particularly inelegant piece of 'ecumenese'—long, lumpish, pretentious, and without joy. The question arises: Is not the reputation of the World Council of Churches being damaged by the quality of some of its publications?

This does not answer the searching question about discipline for sinners' discussion, but—members of the Conference grumbled to one another—it does require us to search for a new discipline which may produce less frustration and more fruit.

V. A UNIQUE RALLY

On the evening of Sunday, July 21st, there took place in the Auditorium of the University of Montreal an ecumenical gathering (in French, *Soirée de Fraternité Chrétienne*) of an unprecedented kind, planned for the Conference by the Montreal Arrangements Committee.

No one presided; there was no platform party or presidium; no benediction was pronounced. On to an empty platform stepped in their turn those who had parts to play. After the Lord's Prayer Dean Stanley B. Frost of McGill University (United Church of Canada) and Father Irénée Beaubien, S.J. (Roman Catholic Church), made speeches of welcome. Dr W. A. Visser 't Hooft in an address on the background of the World Conference on Faith and Order spoke of the 'deep astonishment one must feel at the character of the meeting. It shows that a new beginning is being made. But only a beginning. There remain seemingly unsurpassable obstacles. No serious participant in our movement wants to give up his spiritual integrity or his real convictions. But we all hear the prayer; that they *all* may be one. Not just

c

some, not just *we*, but all, all who bear the name of the Lord Jesus are his disciples.'

In an address entitled 'Toward a Protestant Catholicity', Principal George Johnston (United Church of Canada) spoke of the source of catholicity and the fact of divisiveness in Protestantism and bore witness to the ways in which God has taught Protestants that all who would serve the Lord Christ 'must be Catholic too, in all the range of that magnificent word'. Prayers and anthems, short litanies, Psalms and hymns followed in English and French, Greek, Rumanian and Old Slavonic. Archbishop Athenagoras of Elaia, Greek Orthodox Metropolitan in Canada, spoke on 'Towards a Theology of Unity'. We have lived long in isolation and behind protected walls developed a defensive kind of theology. 'Today a new theology ascends from the depths of our Christian conscience and demands our attention: It is the theology of unity.' With this theology we must analyse that 'blessed inner dissatisfaction' which is the characteristic ecumenical experience: 'It is a sign by which Christ tells us to do something for his suffering and wounded body, the Church.'

Then, after Psalm 46 and *Veni, Sancte Spiritus* had been sung, Cardinal Paul-Emile Léger, Archbishop of Montreal, spoke on 'We are one in Christ'. Having paid tribute to the work of the Faith and Order movement, and quoted the New Delhi statement on the nature of the unity we seek, Cardinal Léger went on to say: 'To answer this unity, we need more than prayers, we need the Holy Eucharist. . . . But the different churches do not have identical notions of the Eucharistic mystery. It is because of these differences that we cannot yet celebrate together the Eucharistic prayer of unity.' Yet the gathering itself, a kind of family reunion, was a sign of hope, however long the way to complete unity with its promise of peace for the world.

After prayers of thanksgiving and penitence, Ezek. 34.11-16 and I John 4.7-11 were read in English, and Matt. 5.1-16 and Phil. 2.5-11 in French, and the Lord's Prayer sung by all three choirs to a Byzantine melody. Prayer for unity was led by the Rt Rev. Kenneth Maguire (Bishop of Montreal in the Anglican Church of Canada) assisted by representatives of various Christian denominations and countries. After which, the people departed in silence.

It is safe to say that no occasion of this sort has ever been held before, anywhere.

VI. GATHERING UP THE THREADS: DECISIONS IN PLENARY SESSION

1. President J. I. McCord presented on behalf of Section IV the document *Communion Services at Ecumenical Gatherings* (pp. 76-80).

The recommendations which it contains recognize with integrity the facts of the present situation and allow for their liturgical expression. Provision is made for an 'open communion'; provision is also made for a 'closed' communion, and formal recognition is also given to the importance for some Christians of the provision of frequent or daily celebrations. In effect, these recommendations imply that all parties are asked to recognize the right to full membership of the ecumenical movement of persons whose eucharistic principles are different from their own, and perhaps abhorrent to them.

Debate centred on recommendation 3—'That arrangements be made within the programme of the conference for one service of Holy Communion according to the liturgy of a church which cannot conscientiously offer an invitation to members of all other churches to partake of the elements. Such a service should be accompanied by an invitation to all the members to be present. Churches sending delegates should encourage them to attend.'

In an eloquent speech Professor W. O. Fennell (United Church of Canada) made a proposal to delete this recommendation, but his motion was defeated by 118 votes to 51 with some abstentions. The discussion tended to assume that the churches referred to would be Orthodox; but there are many Anglicans who hold similar views; and, for other reasons, there are Lutheran and Baptist Churches which do not countenance 'open communion'. And as Fr Bernard Lambert, O.P., stressed in a Section meeting, 'even if the Roman Catholic Church does not belong to the World Council of Churches it does belong to the ecumenical movement'. It is looking some way ahead, perhaps, to expect to see a Roman Catholic Mass 'within the programme'; but not necessarily too far ahead.

There was also debate on a proposal to delete a sentence at the end of recommendation 5 that those whose normal practice is that of frequent or daily communion should give special consideration to their attitude to 'open' services. The sentence in question is somewhat obscure: it might have been better if, for example, it had said 'should consider whether such an early morning service should be held on a Sunday when there is another eucharist within the programme'.

This proposal was heavily defeated; and the recommendations were approved with overwhelming support for transmission to the W.C.C. Central Committee, together with a transcript of the debate.[1]

---

[1] The recommendations, with the important introduction to them, are printed in full on pp. 76–80 in the form in which they were subsequently adopted by the W.C.C. Central Committee at Rochester, New York, in August 1963. The Rochester meeting, while not changing the substance of the Montreal document, made a number of textual alterations in it. As it is the amended version which is issued for general use by the Churches, it seems advisable to avoid confusion by printing that version in this report.—EDITOR.

2. *Pleasant Interlude*

After the coffee-break on the last morning, with the last Section Reports agreed and only *A Word to the Churches* remaining for approval, Archbishop Meliton of Heliopolis, on behalf of the Ecumenical Patriarch, presented gold crosses commemorating the millenary celebrations at Mount Athos to the Bishop of Bristol and to Dr Visser 't Hooft. In graceful replies the recipients dwelt on the long and close connection of the Ecumenical Patriarchate with the Faith and Order Movement and the mutual support which the ministry of the monastic life and the ministry of those who organize conferences can gladly give to each other within the economy of Christ.

3. *A Word to the Churches*[1]

The Bishop of Bristol presented the new draft which had been radically revised after the barrage of criticisms which the hearing on Thursday had directed against the earlier version. (Dr Tomkins had in fact written the new version himself the night before—'as if writing about the Conference as a pastoral letter to my own people'—and had then submitted it to the judgement of his three colleagues, the Vice-chairmen of the Conference.) In the new form, it was at once approved. Fr Sarkissian (Armenian Apostolic Church, Catholicosate of Cilicia) moved that it be sent to the churches not by the officers alone but by the officers on behalf of the Conference; and this also was approved.

4. *Final Reflections and Thanksgivings*

The Bishop of Bristol from the chair expressed the thanks of the Conference to the Theological Commissions on whose work the Conference itself was built. He then went on to speak of the debt to the staff, recalling Dr Oldham's dictum that the ecumenical movement should rightly be traced to its source in Edinburgh 1910 because that Conference for the first time appointed a Continuation Committee and a whole-time staff. He introduced Dr P. S. Minear, who had been Director of the Department during the whole time of the preparation for Montreal, and was now to succeed Dr Douglas Horton as Chairman of the Commission.

Taking his cue from the new terminology employed in Section II, Dr Minear analysed our work profoundly and wittily in term of conference, conferences, and The Conference. In conference, the process of conferencing or conferring, we had had a remarkable success. There had been open vigorous debate between a wide variety of persons, unimpeded by any false respect for persons. Those whose mother tongue was English owed a particular debt of gratitude to the patient efforts of those whose mothers spoke other languages.

[1] For full text, see p. 39.

As one in a series of conferences, this particular conference must recognize failure. We had not solved the problem set us. The Holy Spirit himself had disorganized our plans. We had attempted too much too quickly. We had not found the way to reconcile our conflicting responsibilities—each of us had to speak for his faith, for his confession, for his Section, for the Conference, for the Lord.

But The Conference—the single continuing Conference of God with his people—was beyond success or failure, optimism or pessimism. In this Conference our conference had its goal; and this Conference was also beginning for us now.

Dr Lukas Vischer, Research Secretary of the Department, who spoke in German ('to show that English has not a monopoly'), referred to the mountains of work bequeathed by the Conference before which he felt like the little bird of an Arab fairy tale. At the heart of all these tasks was the continuing effort to embrace a widening company of Christians in an ever more profound dialogue. The effort for a common terminology must be pressed: we must struggle for answers, respecting the word spoken between us. We are like Jacob wrestling for an answer, and there can be no blessing without it. We should watch those question marks: to ask a series of questions could be an ecumenical disease, a way of escape from the demanding discipline of the search for agreement.

The Rev. Patrick C. Rodger reflected, not without wry humour, on the eighteen months' process of conference preparation and the miracle of its happening at all, and reminded us of the relentless pressures of the world which could perhaps produce in scholars (who above all men need peace and quiet for their work) 'a self-pitying resentment that sensitive people should so often be put in a false position'. But did not these pressures upon us reflect the pressures under which the Christian Church must work everywhere in the second half of the twentieth century, and which we may not refuse or evade? He ended with a word of thanks to the chairman—'wise, kindly, patient and decisive, alike in public and in private'—whose leadership of the conference has been characterized by a loving care for all the churches.

The Bishop of Bristol thanked the Conference for their affection; spoke of greetings that had been received from Archbishop Alexis of Tallinn, and from three members of this Conference in the German Democratic Republic who had been unable to receive permission to come. Suitable replies had been sent.

Lastly he expressed the gratitude of the Conference to the Canadian Council of Churches, the Montreal Committee and its sub-committees, McGill University, the Montreal Churches, the Bank of Montreal and several firms who had given services or equipment either free or at greatly reduced cost, the representatives of Television, Radio and the Press, and the conference staff—interpreters, typists, stewards.

Closing Service

On Friday afternoon, July 26th, the Conference met for the last time, in the Anglican Cathedral Church of Christ. The humid heat somewhat reduced the numbers in the procession, but it was not the heat that made the service a fairly short one, but a true perception of the simplicities that need to be expressed in unencumbered fashion at the end of a laborious fortnight. After the splendid hymn (German original by Paul Gerhardt) 'Praise and thanksgiving let all creatures bring' and prayer offered by the Primate of All Canada, Archbishop H. H. Clark, Dr Visser 't Hooft preached on the text (Col. 3.15, N.E.B.) 'Let Christ's peace be arbiter in your hearts: to this you were called as members of a single body. And be filled with gratitude', reminding us of the peace which is God's design, the peace of which all work for unity is a part. Then we sang 'The Church's one Foundation'; Dr V. C. Samuel of the Syrian Orthodox Church of the East led the congregation in a litany; we sang *'Ein' Feste Burg'*; the Archbishop gave the blessing; and the last act of the Conference had taken place.

Evening Prayers, as was noted earlier, had on most days been taken with the help of a booklet, *Let us Pray for Unity*, prepared by Dr J. Robert Nelson, chairman of the Worship Committee. In this booklet the world was divided into ten geographical areas and useful material was provided for intercession in each case. Thus the Conference was encouraged to join in that world-wide prayer for Christian unity, which the Faith and Order Movement had tried for so many years to promote. With the Collect for Unity suggested for daily use, and written by Dr Nelson, this personal and unofficial account may fitly conclude:

> Almighty God our Father, who hast answered the divisive ways of thy rebellious people by offering atonement and unity in thy Son Jesus Christ, so deliver us now from all mutual suspicion, estrangement and bondage to our separate histories, that we may faithfully maintain the unity of thy Spirit and surely come to the oneness in faith, love and witness which thou dost ordain, through Christ our Lord. Amen.

2

A WORD TO THE CHURCHES

from the officers of the
Fourth World Conference on Faith and Order
Montreal, July 1963

1. We are on the way to Christian unity. At Montreal we have seen this afresh because we have been shown that the Lord of all the world is at work, whatever we may do. He is shaping a world which cannot deny that it is one world, except by self-destruction. In that world we Christians find ourselves being drawn and driven together. This is what we mean when we speak of an 'ecumenical reality' which takes shape faster than we can understand or express it.

2. For forty years the Faith and Order movement has been at work to manifest outwardly the unity, which is already ours in Christ, because we have believed that that is God's will. It is increasingly clear that many of our long-defended positions are irrelevant to God's purpose. We still find it hard to know what God calls us to keep or to abandon and what he calls us to venture. But we do know that we must continue to challenge each other in the light of God's will for us.

3. Our task in Faith and Order today is more complex than it ever was. More churches now take part in the conversation, so that new and costly efforts of understanding and imagination are necessary. More parts of the world face difficult and revolutionary situations which raise problems about the role of the churches there. More contact with Roman Catholicism enables us to share in its own self-appraisal, which puts questions to the rest of Christendom. More interests have had to be included in our own agenda, so that we could only touch the fringes of our task.

4. In our Conference we had too much to debate with each other to be able to express a common mind in a single report. So we have forwarded the reports of our five sections to the churches for them to study, knowing that they reflect an experience too varied to be adequately conveyed in print. Yet we, who have been at this Conference, believe that those reports put questions to us as we return to our churches which we would share with you who sent us here.

Will you join us in the attempt to submit all that our own churches mean to us, and all that we can understand of others, to the judgement of Christ, Lord of us all? This conception of our work as a going deep *together* is a new approach and is full of promise.

Will you try to understand other churches' history as deeply as your own? Thus we discover fellowship with other Christians throughout all time as well as throughout all the world. The Church, age-old as well as world-wide, may so learn more of him who is the God of ages.

Will you recognize that Christ calls the whole Church into his whole ministry, so that we may have a fresh understanding of the various ministries which he gives within the whole ministry?

Will you, as you worship God, seek to learn from other traditions more of what true worship is meant to be in all its depth and range, reflecting his presence in remembrance, communion and expectation and magnifying him in the glory and travail of his creation?

Will you humbly recognize that many of God's gifts to his whole Church cannot be shared by us in our local churches, until we become the one people of God in each place, and are prepared to realize this by new and bold ventures of living faith?

5. We do not claim that here we have ourselves faced these questions nearly radically enough, and we are determined to ask them afresh with you. We dare not claim that here we have been truly conscious of such vital issues as the struggle over nuclear armament, bitter racial conflict, scientific technology and social change. Theological debates have an insidious tendency to be self-enclosed. But we pray that our work may indeed be of service to God in his love for all his world, so that the unity of the Church may be not for our sakes but for the sake of him and his children.

6. We invite our churches to continue, in these ways and in every way they can, to manifest openly the unity of life which is hidden with God in Christ. Today we see openings which only faith could discern yesterday. But there is still far to go. Our faith is still in him who is calling us, for he is faithful and he will do it (I Thess. 5.24).

OLIVER TOMKINS   Chairman
Bishop of Bristol

HENRI D'ESPINE

CHRYSOSTOMOS KONSTANTINIDIS   } Vice-Chairmen
Metropolitan of Myra

ALBERT C. OUTLER

3

SECTION REPORTS

SECTION I

'THE CHURCH IN THE PURPOSE OF GOD'

INTRODUCTION

7. The members of this Section unite in confessing the lordship of Jesus Christ. We acknowledge the victory which he won by his cross and which was sealed by his resurrection. In the crucifixion-resurrection we are shown the exacting demands of the obedience to which we are called. We also apprehend the wonder and the power of the divine love (made manifest in Christ), which sustains the Church in suffering and which is the secret of its joy.

8. Within our common affirmation of Christ's lordship we have discovered elements of tension which we neither minimize nor disguise. We gratefully record the vigour and excitement of our debates and we have rejoiced in the stimulus which has come from wrestling with unfamiliar ways of expressing our common faith. From the clash of seemingly conflicting views has come deeper understanding of the inexhaustible riches of the Gospel. Both as individuals and as representatives of traditions we acquiesce too easily in the familiar but often partial statements of the Christian faith to which we are accustomed. One of the great values of meeting others in theological discussion is the challenge which it poses to our customary patterns of thought.

9. Our differences reflect the present ecumenical situation. The growth of the World Council of Churches has enlarged the areas of possible disagreement. We have had to deal honestly with this fact. We have not offered a general pastoral message to the churches. We have not produced a bland synopsis of universally accepted truths. In our report we have pointed to certain questions which, at this point in the churches' history, we have found valuable to explore together. On some subjects we are silent, partly because lack of time prevented us from considering every aspect of a vast theme, but partly because unresolved differences barred the way to an agreed statement. We offer to the churches a brief résumé of the things which we have found

it possible to discuss together, and we hope that other Christians will be encouraged to examine the subjects with which we have wrestled at Montreal.

10. We record with appreciation the contribution which the report *Christ and the Church*[1] has made to Faith and Order studies. This report did not provide us with our detailed agenda but it was the starting-point of our discussions. We believe that it is a useful exploration of the new approach (first suggested by the Lund Conference) to the doctrine of the Church. But this initial effort is unavoidably incomplete. We all record our gratitude for the effort thus far devoted to this enterprise; but some would call in question the emphases which at certain points have emerged. To some members of our Section it seems debatable whether the governing presuppositions of *Christ and the Church* derive from our doctrine of Christ or from our doctrine of the Trinity. Some feel that in so far as a doctrine of Christ has been applied, this doctrine unduly minimizes the significance of the cross. But the report demands further and careful consideration. We have therefore recommended that it be transmitted to the churches for study.

CHRIST, NEW CREATION, CREATION

11. The good news of the Church is that God was in Christ reconciling the world to himself. We therefore confess Jesus Christ as Lord and Saviour in the certainty of his glorious victory over the forces of sin and death. Yet we dare never forget that the Lord of the Church is the 'Lamb with the marks of slaughter upon him' (Rev. 5.6, N.E.B.), i.e., one who for ever remains in his exaltation as the Crucified One. The indivisibility of the crucifixion-resurrection must never be overlooked, nor its significance diminished. Accordingly, the Church must be viewed as the body of the crucified and risen Christ, with an existence determined by participation in the death and resurrection of the Lord who is its head.

12. The Church is the 'new creation' precisely as the body of the crucified-risen Lord. Even as Christ's glory is revealed in his self-humiliation, so in Christ the Church is called and enabled to manifest the 'new creation' in obedient discipleship and faithful servanthood in the world.

13. It is in the response of faith and adoration that the crucified-risen One is proclaimed as Lord and his power is known. But for us in faith to give thanks for his power, to call upon him as our head, is also to have in view the world for which he died. The power of the Crucified One in his glory is exactly the power that enables the Church

[1] See *Faith and Order Findings* (SCM Press, London, 1963, and Augsburg Publishing House, Minneapolis, 1963), Part II, pp. 3-61.

in its lowliness to go into the world and witness to his glory. It is the power of the new creature to obey even to the point of suffering, and the freedom to witness that all rebellious and disobedient powers are subject to the one Lord who has the right of sovereignty over them[1] —though that witness itself bring suffering and humiliation upon the Church.

14. The victory of Christ is realized wherever the freedom of the children of God is given to man. This victory is experienced wherever the people of God are released from the bonds of every enslavement to be truly human, following new paths under the guidance of its Lord. In the grace of God it may be the freedom of a white man and a black man to stand side by side with each other in spite of the world's hostility, a hostility also at work within the churches. It may be the freedom of God's children, in those places where the reality of the cross is daily and openly thrust upon them, to believe and trust in the reign of the risen-crucified Christ over all powers. This freedom also enables us to accept the judgement of the Lord on those of our comfortable churches where the cross has been divorced from discipleship.

15. The freedom of discipleship to the crucified-risen Christ leads to a new solidarity with all God's creatures. The love of Christ which is unconditioned, drives us to identify ourselves with all men, 'good' or 'bad', 'religious' or 'irreligious'. It calls and frees us to be truly men in the secular world of men. Christians are likewise freed to look upon the whole created world as God's good gift which he is bringing to fulfilment through judgement and grace. Christians may gratefully rejoice in all the signs of God's grace and truth in the created order, as well as in all those human achievements through which that order is enabled to express the will and power of God. Together with man, the whole creation has been groaning in travail (Rom. 8.22) and longs to be set free from the powers which still hold it in bondage.[2]

16. QUESTIONS—to be considered in connection with the above: In the Scriptures we read of the glory of the Church as the new

[1] The question of how *Christ's* lordship over the world is to be described was debated extensively. Is it to be identified only with the exercise of his lordship through the Church? Is it a rule *now* exercised even apart from the believing community, and if so, how? How is the tension between the 'already' (Matt. 28.18; Col. 1.15-20; Eph. 1.10, 20-23) and the 'not yet' (I Cor. 15.24; Heb. 2.8; 10.13; Rom. 8.23-24; Col 3.3-4) of Christ's victory to be understood? The Section could not come to any clear resolution of these issues, and believes that their further study in Faith and Order should be encouraged. They are not inter-confessional issues, but they are questions that the churches might profitably explore together.

[2] The whole question of the proper relation of creation and redemption needs much further study in Faith and Order. We are agreed that the grace and power of God is to be found in and received from the world of man outside the Church and in non-human creation. But we are not agreed as to whether or not these are redemptive works of God, or whether or not they should be called works of Christ as marks of his Lordship.

creation and the body of the risen Lord, and of the Christians' participation by their thanksgiving and praise in the victory of Jesus Christ. But what does this glory and participation mean? In our particular times and places, the following are *some* of the ways this question *must* be put to ourselves:

(*a*) If the Church is the body of the crucified Lord, can it ever expect to be more honoured than he?

(*b*) If the glory and victory of the Lord is seen in his being exalted to the cross (John 12.28-33), can the Church attain a greater glory or exhibit a greater power than by following him gladly, even into suffering at the hands of men?

(*c*) If the Church consists of the followers of the Lord who spent his time with publicans and sinners, why does it look so much like a congregation of scribes and pharisees?

(*d*) If the Lord of the Church was crucified outside the camp (Heb. 13.12), why is the Church so often comfortable within its walls and so hesitant to emigrate to new areas in order to risk bearing its witness within endeavours to establish justice and mercy, even where the powers of destruction are at work?

(*e*) How can a church which tolerates the barriers which separate men today, whether east and west or black and white, face its Lord who has broken down the wall of partition (Eph. 2.14)?

(*f*) If Christ has set us free to be truly men, how can we escape solidarity with all men, whether they live as if there were no God or confess him, whether they do good works or live beyond good and evil?

(*g*) If Christ was flesh and blood and if he is to be the Lord of all creation, how can we, his followers, so often flee into a spirituality that divorces God from earth and its possibilities?

THE CHURCH: ACT AND INSTITUTION

17. The Church is founded on the mighty acts of God in calling his chosen people Israel and supremely in his decisive act in the incarnation, suffering, death and resurrection of Jesus Christ, and the sending of the Holy Spirit. Through this total act of God the Church is created as the Body of Christ over which he rules as Head.[1]

18. The Church has its foundation in something that really happened in our world, in the midst of human history. This fact determines the whole life and existence of the Church.

---

[1] The question of God's purpose in the Old Covenant and the New was raised in *Christ and the Church* (p. 40); it emerged also in our discussions, but in a context where extended consideration was impossible. The place of the people of Israel requires careful study, and we strongly recommend that the subject be referred to a commission.

19. The community of the Church was founded to proclaim God's saving act to the world through all ages, and to be continually used by the Spirit to make Christ present again and again through the proclamation of the Word and the administration of the Sacraments. Through these means Christ is always at work afresh through his Spirit, bestowing his salvation on man and calling him to obedient service.

20. The way in which God's decisive action is constantly renewed has been described by the words 'event' and 'institution'. (See *Christ and the Church*, p. 26 ff.) These terms can be criticized; they seem too abstract and impersonal fittingly to describe Christ's Person and his saving work in the Church. But they can also point to the way in which the Church's Lord is, and becomes ever anew, present to his people through the action of the Holy Spirit.

21. The question can be asked whether God is bound to the instruments that he has given and commanded as the means of his presence. We believe that God's command is accompanied by his promise and that he faithfully fulfils that promise by accompanying the obedient use of these given instruments with the free action of his Spirit. Since God's presence is made real to us through instituted means, there must be no playing of charisma and institution against one another.

22. Current ecumenical discussion discloses that the distinction and the relation between event and institution is not a denominational one.

23. The reality that God has given in Jesus Christ through the Holy Spirit is confessed by the Church in terms of its unity, holiness, catholicity and apostolicity. Such is the nature of God's giving and our believing that what is given once and for all is given ever anew and must be received ever anew in the action of God's gracious self-giving and the response of a living faith. So, for example, the Church which *is* one in Jesus Christ *becomes* one in him as it receives in faith the good news of its oneness and seeks to pattern its existence in accordance with its reality. Thus these gifts (unity, holiness, catholicity and apostolicity) are also tasks. In considering the relationship between gift and task, what has been said above concerning event and institution is most relevant.

CHRIST, THE CHURCH AND THE CHURCHES

24. In our discussion of the relation of the churches to the Church we have found it helpful to think not in terms of the churches as parts of the one Church, but rather of the Church as the Body of Christ, including the saints of all ages and the Christians of all places, which is both present in, and one with, the local congregation gathered for the hearing of the Word and the celebration of the Lord's Supper according to Christ's ordinance. 'Wherever Jesus Christ is, there is the Catholic

Church.' Thus each church or congregation participating in Christ is related to others not by participation in some higher structure or organization but rather by an identity of existence in Christ. In this sense each congregation gathered for the proclamation of the Word and the celebration of the Eucharist is a manifestation of the whole Catholic Church in the very process of becoming what she is in service and witness to the world.

25. It must be noted that this formulation refers to the relationship of *congregations* to the Church rather than to that which exists between the 'Churches' (i.e. denominations) and the Church. Some of us would suggest that these denominations themselves be considered primarily as worshipping communities on a different level from the local congregations, but with a similar relationship to the Church in and through their common worship. Others would suggest that they be discussed in terms of their organizational and confessional character. All of us, however, would emphasize the presence of the whole Catholic Church in true Christian worship in such ways that there can be no higher unity than that of which we partake around the Lord's Table, and that every other form of unity can only be justified as an expression of that fundamental unity. This implies that the right of separate ecclesiastical bodies or organizations to continued existence, as well as all movements towards organizational unification, must always be judged anew in the light of that unity and its witness to the world. At various times, groups of Christians have found it imperative to express their faith and worship in particular confessional, national, linguistic, cultural and other associations. We recognize that, under the providence of God, these associations have, in their particular historical situations, often contributed powerfully to the faithful witness of the Church. However, it is clear to us that today God is leading us to be the Church and to bear our witness in unity rather than in separation. In many areas the continuance of the traditional denominational groupings is felt as a scandal. Organizational structures will always be necessary; at the same time we affirm that the unity of the Church is to be found not only in the merger of denominational structures but even more profoundly in the *koinonia* of true eucharistic worship, where the whole Catholic Church is manifested.

26. We should less readily be able to agree on a definition of what constitutes this true eucharistic worship, and therefore to agree about which Christian communities may be regarded as manifestations of the one Church, so that they may be called churches in a more than merely conventional sense. Some would hold that certain Christian communities claiming the name 'church' do not fully manifest the one Church (and some too would add that no community fully manifests the one Church); but all would recognize that in these communities

also Christ is present and his Lordship is acknowledged, and that their members is some sense therefore belong to the one Church.

27. We agree that the criteria for distinguishing a Christian community from a church (in the full sense of the word) are not to be found simply in formal adherence to a creed or confession, submission to a particular hierarchical authority, or possession of a particular ministerial order, but in the nature of its faith and worship and its resultant witness. Therefore it is most important that the aim of all conversation about Faith and Order should be mutual understanding not only in the sphere of doctrine, but also in that of devotion and spirituality, for it is in these fields that there probably lie unrecognized areas both of disagreement and of profound agreement. Such an understanding cannot be reached by any merely superficial comparison of externals, but rather by focusing attention upon the way in which the spirituality of each tradition is related to our common christological and soteriological affirmations.

28. In our discussion of the relation of the churches to one another, we are convinced that the impact of the ecumenical movement and the renewed self-awareness of the churches which this entails must involve profound changes in their thinking and perhaps also in their structure. But we think that much more far-reaching and at present unpredictable consequences for the churches follow from the tremendous revolutions of our time in thought (the dominance of scientific and historical modes of thinking), and in the spheres of society, politics and economics, from the emergence of powerful secularist ideologies, and from the resurgence of non-Christian religions. These pressures are already changing the life of the churches and their relationship to the world in countless ways. Their impact affects not only the individual churches but their relations with one another; and this fact has not been sufficiently taken into account in the ecumenical dialogue. To take one example, the way in which outward circumstances have shaped the practice of inter-church aid ought to have far-reaching implications for our understanding of Christian *diakonia*. In general the reports submitted to this Conference are content to speak of the world as if it were a theological category alone, and not a reality which shapes the Church's witness and through which God addresses the Church. The urgency of this situation calls for immediate thought and action which takes into consideration the freedom of God's initiative working through the various forms and structures of the churches. We do not believe that this task necessitates the establishment of a permanent 'superstructure' over-arching the churches, although the divine freedom may require such structures to be created at certain times for special purposes. In such circumstances it is essential that they be subservient to the one Church as expressed in the churches.

THE CHURCH AND THE WORLD COUNCIL OF CHURCHES

29. The Constitution of Faith and Order stipulates this as one of its functions: 'To study the theological implications of the existence of the ecumenical movement.' At its Third Assembly the World Council of Churches, while affirming that 'the Toronto Statement still best expresses our understanding of the Council's nature', went on to declare that 'the prompting developments of these ten years keep driving us to seek further clarification', and 'the need for careful reflection on the theological meaning of our new life in the Council continues to be unfulfilled.' In the hope of filling this need, the Working Committee of the Faith and Order Commission instructed that this item be placed on the agenda.

30. The Toronto Statement, 1950, addressed itself to this question. It has proved to be very helpful and remains a basic document of the Council. Since then there have been important new developments in the life of the Council:

    (*a*) much increased membership and greater variety of churches;
    (*b*) integration of the International Missionary Council and the World Council of Churches;
    (*c*) the New Delhi Statement on Church Unity;
    (*d*) revision and expansion of the Basis of the Council, 1961;
    (*e*) new avenues of cooperation in inter-church aid;
    (*f*) consideration of the problems of joint action for mission;
    (*g*) relaxation of certain psychological barriers due to better acquaintance and understanding;
    (*h*) reflections on the nature of the Council in the member churches and in our common meetings.

In view of the fast-developing life of the churches acting and thinking together in many realms, we should not proceed without adequate study of the nature of this fellowship. Therefore we find it useful to come to terms with this problem without presuming to give a definitive answer.

31. Member churches attach various meanings to the World Council of Churches. They have different traditions, doctrines and viewpoints concerning the nature of the Church; they use different categories to express these convictions, and so they tend to arrive at different interpretations of the Council.

32. The ecumenical movement is clearly larger than the Council. The World Council of Churches is one of the manifestations of that movement, but there are many other ways through which the churches are growing together.

33. When we speak of 'councils of churches' in English, there is

ambiguity. The Council is of another nature than the ancient ecumenical councils or the councils of the Roman Catholic Church, or the governing council of any other church. (German: *Rat*; French: *conseil*; and both differ from *Konzil* and *concile*.) We have in mind at the same time the councils of churches on city, state, national and international levels. But these also differ in character. Local councils are composed of congregations of denominational bodies, and so cannot avoid restrictions. Some councils purposely avoid the direct discussion of questions of unity, existing only for purposes of cooperation. It may be asked whether any council of churches fulfils its purpose without being concerned deliberately with unity.

34. The mandate to 'study the theological implications of the existence of the ecumenical movement' and 'to reflect on the theological meaning of our new life in the Council' leads us to state that the Council is neither the fulfilment of the hope of unity, nor merely an instrument of cooperation. As a council of churches, or as churches in council, it manifests a growing mutual understanding of the churches and their will to find ultimate unity.

35. The Council is not the Church; it is not seeking to be a church or the Church. Although it has a basis of membership which affirms faith in one God, Father, Son and Holy Spirit, the Council does not assume any ecclesiastical authority, nor does it have sacraments nor an ordained ministry. The Council offers itself as a servant of the churches and of the Church.

36. The Council gratefully acknowledges that in sustained fellowship it has received something new, namely, an enrichment of our Christian existence and a new vision of our common Christian task in the world. The manifestations of this new experience are seen in several ways: a common allegiance to the one Lord; an increasing progress towards a common life of prayer, praise and proclamation; the sharing of burdens, difficulties and pains; and increasing doctrinal consensus without compromise (for example, with regard to the meaning of Baptism); intensified Bible study; the tendencies towards mutual recognition of members among some of the member churches. We do not concur in the precise description of this experience, but we are agreed that it is a new dimension in the Council. We therefore express the ardent wish that this new common experience should grow and increase steadily through God's help and guidance leading us to final unity.

37. Although the present attempt to deal with this problem marks limited progress, further study is necessary. Therefore we express the hope that the Central Committee will give further attention to this matter.

D

Section II

'SCRIPTURE, TRADITION AND TRADITIONS'

INTRODUCTION

38. We find ourselves together in Montreal, delegates of churches with many different backgrounds and many different histories. And yet despite these differences we find that we are able to meet one another in faith and hope in the one Father, who by his Son Jesus Christ has sent the Holy Spirit to draw all men into unity with one another and with him. It is on the basis of this faith and hope, and in the context of a common prayer to the one God, Father, Son and Holy Spirit, that we have studied together anew the problem of the one Tradition and the many traditions, and despite the fact of our separations, have found that we can talk with one another and grow in mutual understanding. The Section warmly commends for study by the churches the Report of the Theological Commission on 'Tradition and Traditions' (*Faith and Order Findings*, Part IV, pp. 3-63), which was the main documentary foundation of its work.

39. In our report we have distinguished between a number of different meanings of the word *tradition*. We speak of the *Tradition* (with a capital T), *tradition* (with a small t) and *traditions*. By *the Tradition* is meant the Gospel itself, transmitted from generation to generation in and by the Church, Christ himself present in the life of the Church. By *tradition* is meant the traditionary process. The term *traditions* is used in two senses, to indicate both the diversity of forms of expression and also what we call confessional traditions, for instance the Lutheran tradition or the Reformed tradition. In the latter part of our report the word appears in a further sense, when we speak of cultural traditions.

40. Our report contains the substance of the work of three subsections. The first considered the subject of the relation of Tradition to Scripture, regarded as the written prophetic and apostolic testimony to God's act in Christ, whose authority we all accept. The concern of the second was with the problem of the one Tradition and the many traditions of Christendom as they unfold in the course of the Church's history. The third discussed the urgent problems raised both in the life of the younger churches and in the churches of the West, concerning the translation of Christian Tradition into new cultures and languages.

41. Part I received a full discussion and the complete approval of the Section. Owing to the lack of time it was not possible to give the same detailed attention to Parts II and III. The Section in general recommends them for study.

I. SCRIPTURE, TRADITION AND TRADITIONS

42. As Christians we all acknowledge with thankfulness that God has revealed himself in the history of the people of God in the Old Testament and in Christ Jesus, his Son, the mediator between God and man. God's mercy and God's glory are the beginning and end of our own history. The testimony of prophets and apostles inaugurated the Tradition of his revelation. The once-for-all disclosure of God in Jesus Christ inspired the apostles and disciples to give witness to the revelation given in the person and work of Christ. No one could, and no one can, 'say that Jesus is Lord, save by the Holy Spirit' (I Cor. 12.3). The oral and written tradition of the prophets and apostles under the guidance of the Holy Spirit led to the formation of Scriptures and to the canonization of the Old and New Testaments as the Bible of the Church. The very fact that Tradition precedes the Scriptures points to the significance of tradition, but also to the Bible as the treasure of the Word of God.

43. The Bible poses the problem of Tradition and Scripture in a more or less implicit manner; the history of Christian theology points to it explicitly. While in the Early Church the relation was not understood as problematical, ever since the Reformation 'Scripture and Tradition' has been a matter of controversy in the dialogue between Roman Catholic and Protestant theology. On the Roman Catholic side, tradition has generally been understood as divine truth not expressed in Holy Scripture alone, but orally transmitted. The Protestant position has been an appeal to Holy Scripture alone, as the infallible and sufficient authority in all matters pertaining to salvation, to which all human traditions should be subjected. The voice of the Orthodox Church has hardly been heard in these Western discussions until quite recently.

44. For a variety of reasons, it has now become necessary to reconsider these positions. We are more aware of our living in various confessional traditions, e.g. that stated paradoxically in the saying 'It has been the tradition of my church not to attribute any weight to tradition.' Historical study and not least the encounter of the churches in the ecumenical movement have led us to realize that the proclamation of the Gospel is always inevitably historically conditioned. We are also aware that in Roman Catholic theology the concept of tradition is undergoing serious reconsideration.

45. In our present situation, we wish to reconsider the problem of Scripture and Tradition, or rather that of Tradition and Scripture. And therefore we wish to propose the following statement as a fruitful way of reformulating the question. Our starting-point is that we are all living in a tradition which goes back to our Lord and has its roots in the Old Testament, and are all indebted to that tradition inasmuch as we

have received the revealed truth, the Gospel, through its being transmitted from one generation to another. Thus we can say that we exist as Christians by the Tradition of the Gospel (the *paradosis* of the *kerygma*) testified in Scripture, transmitted in and by the Church through the power of the Holy Spirit. Tradition taken in this sense is actualized in the preaching of the Word, in the administration of the Sacraments and worship, in Christian teaching and theology, and in mission and witness to Christ by the lives of the members of the Church.

46. What is transmitted in the process of tradition is the Christian faith, not only as a sum of tenets, but as a living reality transmitted through the operation of the Holy Spirit. We can speak of the Christian Tradition (with a capital T), whose content is God's revelation and self-giving in Christ, present in the life of the Church.

47. But this Tradition which is the work of the Holy Spirit is embodied in traditions (in the two senses of the word, both as referring to diversity in forms of expression, and in the sense of separate communions). The traditions in Christian history are distinct from, and yet connected with, the Tradition. They are the expressions and manifestations in diverse historical forms of the one truth and reality which is Christ.

48. This evaluation of the traditions poses serious problems. For some, questions such as these are raised. Is it possible to determine more precisely what the content of the one Tradition is, and by what means? Do all traditions which claim to be Christian contain the Tradition? How can we distinguish between traditions embodying the true Tradition and merely human traditions? Where do we find the genuine Tradition, and where impoverished tradition or even distortion of tradition? Tradition can be a faithful transmission of the Gospel, but also a distortion of it. In this ambiguity the seriousness of the problem of tradition is indicated.

49. These questions imply the search for a criterion. This has been a main concern for the Church since its beginning. In the New Testament we find warnings against false teaching and deviations from the truth of the Gospel. For the post-apostolic Church the appeal to the Tradition received from the apostles became the criterion. As this Tradition was embodied in the apostolic writings, it became natural to use those writings as an authority for determining where the true Tradition was to be found. In the midst of all tradition, these early records of divine revelation have a special basic value, because of their apostolic character. But the Gnostic crisis in the second century shows that the mere existence of apostolic writings did not solve the problem. The question of interpretation arose as soon as the appeal to written documents made its appearance. When the canon of the New Testament had been finally defined and recognized by the Church, it was

still more natural to use this body of writings as an indispensable criterion.

50. The Tradition in its written form, as Holy Scripture (comprising both the Old and the New Testament), has to be interpreted by the Church in ever new situations. Such interpretation of the Tradition is to be found in the crystallization of tradition in the creeds, the liturgical forms of the sacraments and other forms of worship, and also in the preaching of the Word and in theological expositions of the Church's doctrine. A mere reiteration of the words of Holy Scripture would be a betrayal of the Gospel which has to be made understandable and has to convey a challenge to the world.

51. The necessity of interpretation raises again the question of the criterion for the genuine Tradition. Throughout the history of the Church the criterion has been sought in the Holy Scriptures rightly interpreted. But what is 'right interpretation'?

52. The Scriptures as documents can be letter only. It is the Spirit who is the Lord and Giver of life. Accordingly we may say that the right interpretation (taking the words in the widest possible sense) is that interpretation which is guided by the Holy Spirit. But this does not solve the problem of criterion. We arrive at the quest for a hermeneutical principle.

53. This problem has been dealt with in different ways by the various churches. In some confessional traditions the accepted hermeneutical principle has been that any portion of Scripture is to be interpreted in the light of Scripture as a whole. In others the key has been sought in what is considered to be the centre of Holy Scripture, and the emphasis has been primarily on the Incarnation, or on the Atonement and Redemption, or on justification by faith, or again on the message of the nearness of the Kingdom of God, or on the ethical teachings of Jesus. In yet others, all emphasis is laid upon what Scripture says to the individual conscience, under the guidance of the Holy Spirit. In the Orthodox Church the hermeneutical key is found in the mind of the Church, especially as expressed in the Fathers of the Church and in the Ecumenical Councils. In the Roman Catholic Church the key is found in the deposit of faith, of which the Church's *magisterium* is the guardian. In other traditions again the creeds, complemented by confessional documents or by the definitions of Ecumenical Councils and the witness of the Fathers, are considered to give the right key to the understanding of Scripture. In none of these cases where the principle of interpretation is found elsewhere than in Scripture is the authority thought to be alien to the central concept of Holy Scripture. On the contrary, it is considered as providing just a key to the understanding of what is said in Scripture.

54. Loyalty to our confessional understanding of Holy Scripture

produces both convergence and divergence in the interpretation of Scripture. For example, an Anglican and a Baptist will certainly agree on many points when they interpret Holy Scripture (in the wide sense of interpretation), but they will disagree on others. As another example, there may be mentioned the divergent interpretations given to Matt. 16.18 in Roman Catholic theology on the one hand, and in Orthodox or Protestant theology on the other. How can we overcome the situation in which we all read Scripture in the light of our own traditions?

55. Modern biblical scholarship has already done much to bring the different churches together by conducting them towards the Tradition. It is along this line that the necessity for further thinking about the hermeneutical problem arises: i.e. how we can reach an adequate interpretation of the Scriptures, so that the Word of God addresses us and Scripture is safeguarded from subjective or arbitrary exegesis. Should not the very fact that God has blessed the Church with the Scriptures demand that we emphasize more than in the past a common study of Scripture whenever representatives of the various churches meet? Should we not study more the Fathers of all periods of the Church and their interpretations of the Scriptures in the light of our ecumenical task? Does not the ecumenical situation demand that we search for the Tradition by re-examining sincerely our own particular traditions?

II. THE UNITY OF TRADITION AND THE DIVERSITY OF TRADITIONS

56. Church and tradition are inseparable. By tradition we do not mean traditionalism. The Tradition of the Church is not an object which we possess, but a reality by which we are possessed. The Church's life has its source in God's act of revelation in Jesus Christ, and in the gift of the Holy Spirit to his people and his work in their history. Through the action of the Holy Spirit, a new community, the Church, is constituted and commissioned, so that the revelation and the life which are in Jesus Christ may be transmitted to the ends of the earth and to the end of time. The Tradition in its content not only looks backward to its origin in the past but also forward to the fulness which shall be revealed. The life of the Church is lived in the continuous recalling, appropriation and transmission of the once-for-all event of Christ's coming in the flesh, and in the eager expectation of his coming in glory. All this finds expression in the Word and in the Sacraments in which 'we proclaim the Lord's death till he come' (I Cor. 11.26).

57. There are at least two distinctive types of understanding of the Tradition. Of these, the first is affirmed most clearly by the Orthodox. For them, the Tradition is not only the act of God in Christ, who comes by the work of the Holy Spirit to save all men who believe in him; it is also the Christian faith itself, transmitted in wholeness and purity,

and made explicit in unbroken continuity through definite events in the life of the catholic and apostolic Church from generation to generation. For some others, the Tradition is substantially the same as the revelation in Christ and the preaching of the Word, entrusted to the Church which is sustained in being by it, and expressed with different degrees of fidelity in various historically conditioned forms, namely the traditions. There are others whose understanding of the Tradition and the traditions contain elements of both these points of view. Current developments in biblical and historical study, and the experience of ecumenical encounter, are leading many to see new values in positions which they had previously ignored. The subject remains open.

58. In the two distinctive positions mentioned above, the Tradition and the traditions are clearly distinguished. But while in the one case it is held that it is to be found in the organic and concrete unity of the one Church, in the other it is assumed that the one Tradition can express itself in a variety of forms, not necessarily all equally complete. The problem of the many churches and the one Tradition appears very differently from each of those points of view. But though on the one side it is possible to maintain that the Church cannot be, and has not been, divided, and on the other to envisage the existence of many churches sharing in the one Tradition even though not in communion with each other, none would wish to acquiesce in the present state of separation.

59. Many of our misunderstandings and disagreements on this subject arise out of the fact of our long history of estrangement and division. During the centuries the different Christian communions have developed their own traditions of historical study and their own particular ways of viewing the past. The rise of the idea of a strictly scientific study of history, with its spirit of accuracy and objectivity, in some ways ameliorated this situation. But the resultant work so frequently failed to take note of the deeper theological issues involved in church history, that its value was severely limited. More recently, a study of history which is ecumenical in its scope and spirit has appeared.

60. We believe that if such a line of study is pursued, it can be of great relevance to the present life and problems of the Church: 'those who fail to comprehend their histories are doomed to re-enact them' (Santayana). We believe, too, that it would have great value in offering possibilities of a new understanding of some of the most contested areas of our common past. We therefore specifically recommend that Faith and Order should seek to promote such studies, ensuring the collaboration of scholars of different confessions, in an attempt to gain a new view of crucial epochs and events in church history, especially those in which discontinuity is evident.

61. But at this point another problem arises. At a moment when mankind is becoming ever more aware of itself as a unity, and we are faced with the development of a global civilization, Christians are called to a new awareness of the universality of the Church, and of its history in relation to the history of mankind. This means that, both at the level of theological study and of pastoral teaching, an attempt has to be made to overcome the parochialism of most studies in church history, and to convey some idea of the history of God's people as a whole. But how is this to be done? Does it not demand the work of historians with more than human capabilities? Is it possible for the scholar, limited as he is by his own cultural, historical and ecclesiastical background, to achieve this vision? Clearly it is not, though we believe that by working in collaboration something could be accomplished. For specialized but limited insights and points of view can be checked and supplemented by those of others; for example, a group may command a larger number of languages and literatures than is possible for an individual. Questions are being raised in the philosophy and theology of history, pointing both to the danger of mere traditionalism and the permanent value of authentic traditionalism. These demand our constant consideration.

62. Still a third kind of historical concern has been with us. We are aware that during the period of this Conference we have been passing through a new and unprecedented experience in the ecumenical movement. For the first time in the Faith and Order dialogue, the Eastern Orthodox and the other Eastern Churches have been strongly represented in our meetings. A new dimension of Faith and Order has opened up, and we only begin to see its future possibilities. It is clear that many of our problems of communication have arisen from the inadequate understanding of the life and history of the Eastern Churches to be found even among scholars in the West, and *vice versa*. Here again is an area in which we would recommend further study, e.g. of the problem of the *filioque*, its origin and consequences. There are two other studies which we recommend to the Faith and Order Commission. We believe it important to undertake together a study of the Councils of the Early Church, and we recommend an examination of the catechetical material at present in use by the churches, and of the methods whereby it could be revised in the light of the ecumenical movement.

63. In all this we are not blind to the nature of the world in which we live, nor to the cultural and intellectual problems of our day. To many of our contemporaries a concern with the past will immediately appear suspect, as revealing a desire for the mere resuscitation of old customs and ideas, which have no relevance for the urgent questions of our time. We recognize that in many places human traditions—national, social, and indeed religious—are being shaken; and that in this age of

scientific and technological achievement many tend to regard the heritage of the past as unimportant. We recognize the positive elements in the present situation. It is for this reason that we have placed the contrast of tradition and traditionalism at the beginning of this part. The past of which we speak is not only a subject which we study from afar. It is a past which has value for us, in so far as we make it our own in an act of personal decision. In the Church it becomes a past by which we live by sharing in the one Tradition, for in it we are united with him who is the Lord of history, who was and is and is to come; and he is God not of the dead but of the living.

III. THE CHRISTIAN TRADITION AND CULTURAL DIVERSITY

64. In what has been written so far, we have been concerned primarily with the understanding of Tradition as it relates to the past, to the once-for-all event of Christ's coming in the flesh, his death and resurrection, and to the continuing work of the Holy Spirit within the Church. But we have recognized throughout, that Tradition looks also to the present and to the future. The Church is sent by Christ to proclaim the Gospel to all men; the Tradition must be handed on in time and also in space. In other words, Tradition has a vital missionary dimension in every land, for the command of the Lord is to go to all nations. Whatever differences of interpretation there may be, all are agreed that there is this dynamic element in the Tradition, which comes from the action of God within the history of his people and its fulfilment in the person and work of Christ, and which looks to the consummation of the victory of the Lord at the end of time.

65. The problems raised by the transmission of the Tradition in different lands and cultures, and by the diversities of traditions in which the one Tradition has been transmitted, are common in varying ways to all Christians. They are to be seen in an acute form in the life of the younger churches of Asia and Africa today, and in a less obvious but no less real form in what was formerly called Western Christendom. To take the problem of the younger churches, in one quite small and typical country there are more than eighty different denominations. How among these traditions are we to find the Tradition? In the building up of new nations there is a particular need for all that will make for unity among men. Are Christians, to whom the ministry of reconciliation has been committed, to be a factor of division at such a time? It is in such testing circumstances as these that the serious problems have to be faced of how the Church may become truly indigenous, bringing into the service of Christ all that is good in the life of every culture and nation, without falling into syncretism.

66. When the Word became flesh, the Gospel came to man through a particular cultural medium, that of the Palestinian world of the time.

So when the Church takes the Tradition to new peoples, it is necessary that again the essential content should find expression in terms of new cultures. Thus in the great missionary expansion of the Eastern Church, the Tradition was transmitted through the life of the Church into new languages and cultures, such as those of Russia and the other mission fields. Just as the use of the Slavonic tongue was necessary for the transmission of the Tradition to the Slavs, so today it is necessary to use new languages and new forms of expression which can be understood by those to whom the good news comes. In order that this can be rightly done, it is necessary to draw together knowledge of the culture and language in question, along with a careful study of the languages of the Old and New Testaments, and a thorough knowledge of church history. It is in this context that we begin to understand the meaning of the gift of tongues at Pentecost. By the power of the Holy Spirit the apostles were enabled to preach the mighty works of God to each man in his own tongue, and thus the diversity of nations and cultures was united in the service of God. Through recognizing this, Christians in countries where they are a small minority can avoid the dangers of developing a 'ghetto mentality'.

67. The content of the Tradition cannot be exactly defined, for the reality it transmits can never be fully contained in propositional forms. In the Orthodox view, Tradition includes an understanding of the events recorded in the New Testament, of the writings of the Fathers, of the ecumenical creeds and Councils, and of the life of the Church throughout the centuries. All member churches of the World Council of Churches are united in confessing the Lord Jesus Christ 'as God and Saviour, according to the Scriptures, and in seeking together to fulfil their common calling to the glory of the one God, Father, Son and Holy Spirit'. This basis of membership safeguards a position from which we may seek constantly to grow in understanding of the fulness of God's revelation, and to correct partial apprehensions of the truth. In the task of seeking to understand the relation between the Tradition and the traditions, problems are raised as difficult to solve as they are crucial in importance. Such questions often cannot be answered apart from the specific situations which pose them. There are no ready-made solutions. Yet some things may be said.

68. What is basic in the Old and New Testament record and interpretation remains basic for the Church in any situation. Moreover, the Holy Spirit has been given to the Church to guide it into all truth. The decisions which communities of God's believing people have to take are to be made in reliance on this leading of his Spirit within the Church, and in awareness of God's providential operations in the world. In the process of indigenization (understood in its widest sense), nothing can be admitted which is at variance with the good news of

what God has done, is doing and will do, in the redemption of the world through our Lord Jesus Christ, as expressed in terms of the Church's christocentric and trinitarian faith. In each particular situation, the Gospel should be so proclaimed that it will be experienced, not as a burdensome law, but as a 'joyful, liberating and reconciling power'. The Church must be careful to avoid all unnecessary offence in the proclamation of its message, but the offence of the cross itself, as foolishness to the world, can never be denied. And so the attempt must always be made to transmit the Tradition in its fulness and to remain within the community of the whole of God's people, and the temptation must be avoided of over-emphasizing those elements which are especially congenial to a particular culture. It is in the wholeness of God's truth that the Church will be enabled to fulfil its mission and to bear authentic witness.

69. The traditionary process involves the dialectic, both of relating the Tradition as completely as possible to every separate cultural situation in which men live, and at the same time of demonstrating its transcendence of all that divides men from one another. From this comes the truth that the more the Tradition is expressed in the varying terms of particular cultures, the more will its universal character be fully revealed. It is only 'with all the saints' that we come to know the fulness of Christ's love and glory (Eph. 3.18-19).

70. Catholicity, as a gift of God's grace, calls us to a task. It is a concept of immense richness whose definition is not attempted here. It can be sought and received only through consciousness of, and caring for, the wholeness of Christ's body, through witness for Christ's lordship over every area of human life, and through compassionate identification with every man in his own particular need.

71. In the fulfilment of their missionary task most churches claim not merely to be reproducing themselves, but in some sense to be planting the *una sancta ecclesia*. Surely this fact has implications which are scarcely yet realized, let alone worked out, both for the life of the mother-churches, and also for all that is involved in the establishing of any new church in an ecumenical age. It demands that the liberty of newly-founded churches be recognized, so that both mother- and daughter-churches may receive together the one gift of God's grace. This demands faithfulness to the whole *koinonia* of Christ's Church, even when we are engaged with particular problems. In this connection we recognize a vital need for the study of the history of the Church's life and mission, written from an ecumenical perspective. All must labour together in seeking to receive and manifest the fulness of Christ's truth.

72. The problem of communicating this fulness of truth today is felt throughout the whole modern world. This is a result of the emer-

gence in our time of a global civilization, shaped by rapid technological advances, and grounded in a scientific outlook that transforms our concept of the universe. The new cosmology which is taking shape challenges our traditional conceptions of man and of nature, both in themselves and in their inter-relationship with one another. Amid these developments, and to some degree because of them, radical changes in social structure are taking place in every part of the world. The Church is thus faced with a dual responsibility. The Tradition has to be simultaneously transmitted in diverse ways; on the one hand, in popular everyday language; on the other hand, in terms of the most complex and critical contemporary thought. The seriousness of this revolutionary situation cannot easily be exaggerated. We have seen its inherent dangers, but we must equally seek to realize its enormous potentialities for good.

73. Our thinking about the Christian faith too often lacks a forward-looking vision and orientation. The phrase '*in partibus infidelium*' has already acquired a universal reference. Experiments in pastoral and evangelistic work, such as industrial chaplaincies and 'store front parishes', are first attempts at meeting this need. The deepest witness is always borne by the life of the Church itself, through its prayer and sacramental worship, and through the bearing of the cross in silence. As we address ourselves together to our common problems, we may find that God is using the pressures of the world to break the barriers which divide us from one another. We must recognize the opportunity given to us, and with vigour and boldness fulfil the Church's great commission to transmit the Tradition, the word of grace and hope, to men in this new global culture, as in the past it was preached to Jerusalem, to Hellas, Rome and Gaul, and to the uttermost parts of the earth.

APPENDIX

74. The document presented to the Section on 'The Revision of Catechisms in the Light of the Ecumenical Movement' contains a number of important proposals which are highly relevant to our work on Tradition and traditions. Catechetical instruction or religious education is obviously one important way in which the traditionary process works, for the instruction of the young is a continual effort at indigenization in each new generation. There are many questions which the churches ought to address to themselves about the effectiveness and fidelity of their catechisms and other teaching materials as instruments of the traditionary process. We confine ourselves however to one main question: How far do the teaching materials which are used in our churches reflect their ecumenical commitments and intentions? Negatively stated the question would be: How far do these teaching

materials reflect prejudices and misunderstandings which we ought to have outgrown, and perhaps thought that we had outgrown?

75. Before this question can be adequately answered, a detailed analysis of what actually happens in our churches must be made. This is a modest proposal, but it seems to have these advantages: it could lead quickly to practical decision and action; it could involve people who do not normally share actively in the life of the ecumenical movement; and it could directly affect many members of the churches.

76. We therefore propose that these four questions be addressed to the churches:

(*a*) What statements of ecumenical intention has your church issued? What are the ecumenical commitments which your church has undertaken? How are these intentions and commitments reflected in your educational materials, e.g. catechisms which are teaching instruments, Sunday-school lessons and textbooks?

If your church has entered into fellowship with other churches in the W.C.C., or is engaged in conversations with other churches, how is this fact reflected in such materials?

(*b*) How do your educational materials deal with the dilemma created by the fact that we acknowledge one Baptism into Christ and yet live as separated churches?

(*c*) How are the other Christian bodies described in your educational materials? Is the description accurate and fair? Would the other churches recognize themselves in the picture you draw of them?

(*d*) What proportion of time is spent on teaching our common faith and our common history as Christians, and what proportion on teaching that history and doctrine which distinguishes your church from other churches?

SECTION III

'THE REDEMPTIVE WORK OF CHRIST AND THE MINISTRY OF HIS CHURCH'

INTRODUCTION

77. Ministry and order have not been on the agenda of a World Faith and Order Conference since Edinburgh 1937. Section III at Montreal has been given the task of discussing again, after this interval, our understanding of the place of ministers of Jesus Christ in the life of the Church. During these twenty-five years there has been a notable

recovery of the biblical teaching about the royal priesthood of the whole people of God. There have been times in the past when the word 'layman' was understood to refer to someone who had a merely passive role in the life of the Church, and the word 'ministry' referred exclusively to the full-time professional service of the Church. That time is past. A recovery of a true doctrine of the laity has brought with it the recognition that ministry is the responsibility of the whole body and not only of those who are ordained. This recovery is one of the most important facts of recent church history, and we express our gratitude in this connection for the work of the Department on the Laity of the World Council of Churches, and especially for the paper entitled *Christ's Ministry and the Ministry of the Church* (Laity Bulletin No. 15, available from the W.C.C.) which has been the starting-point of our discussion.

78. It is a significant fact that the work of the Laity Department led it to raise the question of the function and authority of the ordained ministry, and it is with this question that we have tried to deal, even though the title given to us, if strictly interpreted, refers to the whole work of the Church in the world. We agree with the Department on the Laity that the narrower question can only be answered in the context of the broader, and we have tried always to bear this context in mind. But we confess frankly that we have not attempted to deal with the total ministry of the Church in the world. For this we refer again to the work of the Laity Department.

79. Any fuller account of the doctrine of the ministry would have to be placed within the context of man's total existence in the world of which Christ is Redeemer and Lord.

80. In addressing ourselves to the narrower question we have faced difficulties even in defining our subject. We all acknowledge that the Church has always had and (so far as we know) always must have what we may call 'a special ministry'. But there is no universally agreed language by which to describe this special ministry in distinction from the ministry of the Church as a whole. There is no agreement as to the relation and distinction between them, and there is no agreement as to what is, and what is not, included in the 'special ministry'. Even a preliminary definition of terms implies some provisional opinion on questions of substance. Not merely in spite of, but precisely because of, this confusion we believe that the time is ripe to study afresh the special ministry of those who are ordained to be the servants of the servants of God, and its relation to the general ministry of all Christian people.

81. Recognizing the many unresolved differences of belief among us, we believe we ought to approach this question in the first place not merely by comparing our different confessional views, but by seeking to penetrate 'behind our divisions to a deeper and richer understanding

of the mystery of the God-given unity of Christ with His Church' (Lund Report). In this report we invite member churches to start to think together again about the special ministry, and we propose the following brief theses for study.

82. For the purpose of the present document we have agreed to use the words 'special ministry' and 'ministers' to describe that which is the focal concern of our study.

THE WORK OF CHRIST AND THE MISSION OF THE CHURCH

83. The redemptive work of Christ has its origin in the mission given by the Father to the Son, and willed by the Son with the Father in the Holy Spirit. In accordance with the purpose of God, prepared and foretold under the covenant with Israel, and by the power of the Holy Spirit, the Son became man, proclaimed the Kingdom of God with power, was crucified, died, rose again, and lives eternally as Lord. In this Person, this history and this work, God was in Christ, reconciling the world to himself. That which the Lord Jesus Christ has thus accomplished, he has accomplished once for all.

84. In order that his redemptive work might be proclaimed and attested to the ends of the earth, and that its fruits might be communicated to man, Christ chose apostles, witnesses of his resurrection, and committed to them the word of reconciliation. Having clothed them with the Holy Spirit he sent them to gather all nations into the Church and to build it upon the one foundation which is no other than himself, and to inaugurate the ministry of the accomplished reconciliation for the salvation of all men. Thus the whole Church and its special ministry have their origin in the sending of the apostles.

85. The unique witness of the apostles to Christ is preserved by the Church in the New Testament. Their mission is continued by the Church and in its ministry.

86. The Church, the people chosen by God, is the community of those who have been gathered in faith by the apostolic preaching and by the power of the Spirit and have been plunged into the waters of baptism. It belongs to Christ, as his own body confesses him, worships him and obeys him, as the redeemer of the world. Taken from the world and set in the world, it constitutes there the royal priesthood declaring the wonderful deeds of God, and offering to him as a sacrifice both worship and daily life.

87. In order to build up the Church and to equip it for its mission, the Lord Jesus Christ has given ministers who, following the apostles and by the power of the Spirit, serve the accomplished reconciliation in, with, and for the body by announcing, attesting and communicating that reconciliation by the means which the Lord has given.

CHRIST, THE CHURCH AND THE SPECIAL MINISTRY

88. All ministry in the Church is rooted in the ministry of Christ himself, who glorifies the Father in the power of the Holy Spirit. Christ stirs up, calls, strengthens and sends those whom he has chosen for the whole ministry of his Church and for the special ministry, making them the instrument of his message and of his work. Ministers are called to serve the work of the Lord by following him, by being conformed to him, and by announcing his name.

89. The special ministry thus reflects and serves the redemptive love of Christ.

(a) Christ is Prophet; his Church is called to be his witness, announcing to the world by word and deed the good news of the Word made flesh, of the accomplished reconciliation, and of the Kingdom which comes. That it may truly be so, the ministers are set in its midst to proclaim him.

(b) Christ is High Priest; his Church is called to be the true priesthood in the world, holding out to all men the gift of the reconciliation which he has purchased, and offering up on behalf of all men both the sacrifice of praise, thanksgiving and obedience, and the prayer of penitence and intercession. That it may truly be so, the ministers are set for the priestly service of the Gospel in the midst of the priestly people.

(c) Christ is King; his whole Church is called to be the sign of his Kingdom in the midst of the world, the evidence to men that the devil is conquered and that God reigns. That it may truly be so, the ministers are set in the midst to be the servants of the King, guarding his people in their unity one with another and with him, leading them in their spiritual warfare, and equipping them with all the armour of God.

In these ways the ministers are the servants of the Servant of God, and thus share in his suffering and in his joy.

90. This ministry of Jesus Christ in his Church is made effective by the action of the Holy Spirit promised by the Lord to his people. To serve Christ in his Church means to wait always upon the Spirit of power, holiness and love. It is in this waiting upon the Spirit that the ministers of the Church preach the word, administer the sacraments, watch in prayer, lead God's people, and engage in deeds of brotherly help. In dependence upon the same Spirit the whole Church shares the responsibility for this stewardship of the riches of Christ.

91. The whole Church receives and supports those who have been given to it for the ordering of its mission, and they depend upon the spiritual gifts, the prayers and the generosity of the whole fellowship.

Thus the whole body standing firm together is armed for its service.

THE SPIRIT, THE MINISTRIES AND THE SPECIAL MINISTRY

92. The Holy Spirit dwells in the Church. He comes to each member in his baptism for the quickening of faith. He also bestows differing gifts (*charismata*) on groups and individuals. All his activities are to enable men to serve and worship God. All members of the Church are thus gifted for the common good.

93. The Spirit equips God's people in a threefold way:

(*a*) He enables them as children of their heavenly Father to live and work in the world without faithless anxiety. There they find their principal place of testimony and their principal sphere of service. There they live as first fruits of a new creation.

(*b*) The Spirit builds up the body of Christ in love, truth and holiness, by equipping the members with the manifold and varied gifts which they need for the service of one another and for the mission of the Church.[1]

(*c*) Among the differing gifts bestowed by the Spirit is the special ministry.

THE CALL AND AUTHORIZATION OF THE MINISTER

94. The call to the special ministry depends upon the presence and the action of the Holy Spirit in the Church. He is at the same time a free Spirit choosing whom he will, and an ever-present Spirit guaranteeing to the Church that God does not cease to call men into the service of the Lord and to give them necessary gifts. He leads the Church to seek out and to recognize the presence amongst her members of these gifts and this calling, and to test the gift and the calling given to men by God. The divine initiative may make use of the voice of the community or may be addressed individually to the Christian. In any case the exercise of the special ministry in the Church requires the acknowledgement and the confirmation of the Church.

95. This confirmation is given in ordination. According to the New Testament, this ordination consists in prayer with the laying on of hands. The orderly transmission of authority in ordination is normally an essential part of the means by which the Church is kept from generation to generation in the apostolic faith. All of us regard this continuity in the apostolic faith as essential to the Church. Some of us, including the Orthodox, believe that the unbroken succession of episcopal ordination from the apostles is a necessary guarantee of a

---

[1] We propose that the question of the diaconate and that of the ordination of women receive further attention in Faith and Order.

E

valid ministry and of the safeguarding of the true faith, and that ordination is itself a sacrament. Others among us believe that it is the work of the Holy Spirit not only to preserve order in the Church but also to create new forms of order when existing forms have ceased to safeguard the true faith. Some believe that there is not sufficient authority in the New Testament to warrant the practice of ordination in the sense of setting men apart for a life-ministry in the Church. We recognize the gravity of these differences. At the same time we are all agreed in accepting the statement of the Third Assembly that the unity which we seek includes a ministry accepted and acknowledged by all. There are differences of belief and practice among us on what constitutes the special ministry. Some churches recognize seven orders in the special ministry, some three, some only one. But the threefold pattern (bishop, presbyter, deacon) is also found (e.g. in the form of pastor, elder, deacon) in churches which normally speak of only one order in the special ministry. There is need both for discussion between the churches about these differing traditions, and also for self-examination within our churches about the way in which we have received and used the gift of ministry. For example, we must ask ourselves such questions as the following:

(*a*) Granted that there is an essential ministry given to the Church by the Lord, does the traditional pattern of ministry in our churches do justice to the variety of the gifts of the Spirit?

(*b*) Have churches which follow the pattern 'bishop, priest, deacon' in fact preserved the specific character of each of these orders of ministry as taught in their formularies? Do churches which have the pattern 'pastor, elder, deacon' (or some similar pattern) preserve the ministerial character of each? On what theological principles are elders (presbyters) or deacons included in, or excluded from, the special ministry?

(*c*) While in all our churches men and women are set aside for limited periods for some forms of ministry, ordination to the special ministry is almost universally regarded as being for life. What are the grounds for this?

(*d*) The following qualifications for the special ministry have by no means always been regarded as indispensable: academic training, full-time service, salary. Are they treated as indispensable in our churches today, and if so, on what grounds? How are these aspects of the ministry related to the fundamental theology of the ministry?

THE MINISTER, THE CHURCH AND THE WORLD

96. The minister, like the apostle, is sent to the world to show forth by word and deed the dying and resurrection of Jesus Christ, and is

also given to the Church to remind it of that dying and rising by which it lives, and which it has to communicate to the world.

97. The minister is sent to the world in which and for which Christ died. There he may be called to share the apostolic sufferings; afflictions, hardships, calamities. Certainly, he will share in the apostolic labours. He goes into the world on behalf of Christ, speaking to a divided and estranged mankind the word of reconciliation. In this obedience he will share in the apostolic joy.

98. The special responsibility committed to the minister in the Church is the equipment of the other members in the work of ministry that they may carry out the responsibility committed to them in baptism. This will call for a constant ministry of preaching, teaching and pastoral care. Ministers are given to the Church as the Lord's messengers, watchmen and stewards, and as such they have to give an account to him of their stewardship.

THE SPECIAL MINISTRY IN TODAY'S WORLD

99. All baptized Christians are called to respond to, and participate in, the ministry of Christ directed toward the world. 'He calls his Church to embody his ministry of reconciliation in its life as well as in its proclamation' (Report on 'Christ and the Church', *Faith and Order Findings*, Part II, p. 56). Here we recognize the incalculable importance of the ministry of those members of the body who make constantly visible the presence of the Church in the midst of the world.

100. In the changing world in which we live, the existing forms of ministry of the Church must be re-examined. This should be done not so that the ministry is conformed to the world, but that it may manifest the essential character of the ministry of Christ in the changing patterns of society. In speaking of 'forms' in this section we are not touching at all upon such matters of fundamental tradition as—for example—the threefold order of the ministry in some churches; we are concerned with the changing place of the minister in society.

101. Churches faced with rapidly changing situations are struggling to find forms of ministry relevant to their situation, and this not by abandoning traditional forms of the special ministry, but by seeking to give a diversity and flexibility such as we recognize in the New Testament and in the Church of the first centuries.

(a) In many parts of Asia and Africa, in the past, the traditional Western forms of the special ministry have often been preserved in all their institutional rigidity. This has led to the serious results of leaving many congregations in those areas virtually without sacramental life because they cannot support an ordained pastor, and of forming congregations whose energies are more introverted than directed toward strengthening the Church's service and witness in the world. The Church has appeared as an institution centred in a building, rather than as a company moving out into the world.

(*b*) In many parts of the world, the traditional settled parish-congregation of recent centuries has been changing rapidly. When there is a rapid development of urban and industrial society with its mobility of population and diversity of life, pastors serving within the existing parochial system find it increasingly difficult to minister effectively to the real communities in which men live and make their crucial decisions. In these cases there is need of new patterns of the special ministry; more dynamic. flexible, and relevant to the situation in which the ministry is at work.

102. There are several possibilities of more flexible forms of ministry in the light of experiments, for example:

(*a*) The Church may ordain a man who works in a secular employment but has shown pastoral gifts. He will serve the local congregation as a pastor, while continuing his secular work as e.g. farmer or village teacher.

(*b*) In some sectors of society which are impenetrable to existing forms of ministry (such as certain areas of industrial life, where groups of Christians are learning to work and witness in terms of the conditions of life there), the best way to ensure the full witness of the Gospel may be to ordain members of these groups to the ministry of word and sacraments after appropriate training, so that they may build up the body of Christ without being 'professional clergy'.

(*c*) In a frontier situation, where there is no Christian community among the people, the Church may select a minister and send him into some secular employment so that he becomes a part of the community and within it seeks to witness and to form the community of God's people, the Church.

(*d*) In highly specialized or diversified societies, the Church may consider the possibility of assigning to the professionally trained ordained minister a specific role to strengthen the witness and service of God's people in a particular sector of society, e.g. among industrial workers or other professional groups.

(*e*) In many pioneer situations in industrial and urban society a team ministry crossing denominational lines has been formed. Such a group ministry can be, within modern society, a visible manifestation of the solidarity of God's people. Thus the Church can perform a service among the people of today who genuinely seek fellowship in their perplexity and loneliness.

(*f*) In certain situations an itinerant ministry has enabled the Church to respond effectively to rapidly changing conditions.

103. When the Church is thus involved in a frontier situation, the question of unity becomes even more urgent. In cases of extreme need churches have learned the necessity and the blessing of inter-confessional assistance. Here again we recognize the insistence of God's calling of the Church into visible unity which alone can provide a unified ministry really effective in the new and revolutionary world in which we find ourselves.

104. The Church with all her ministries lives continuously in history as a pilgrim people among all the communities of mankind, in obedience to Christ and in a constant solidarity with the world. This means that the Church responds to the suffering and victorious ministry of Christ with repentance and renewal, with the hope and joy which Jesus gives, always ready to be reshaped in the forms of its ministry according to his call at each stage of the pilgrim life.

Section IV

'WORSHIP AND THE ONENESS OF CHRIST'S CHURCH'

I. THE NATURE OF CHRISTIAN WORSHIP

105. We believe that Christian worship is deeply relevant for the daily life of men in this present age. At the same time, we realize that the liturgical forms and language of the churches, including that of preaching, are everywhere in need of transformation. In both respects, we, who have come together from all parts of the world and from virtually all the prominent traditions of the Church, have reached what is to us a remarkable consensus. We have found much agreement on what constitutes Christian worship and upon the value of the particular emphases which each of our liturgical traditions has contributed. Yet we have also been compelled to agree that these traditions are inadequate for the current mission of the Church. A proper indication of this consensus is scarcely possible within the allotted scope of this report. However, we believe we can point to a certain direction in which the Spirit may be moving the churches today.

106. Among the many recent blessings of the ecumenical movement, one in particular is of decisive importance for the common mission of the churches in our time. It is the current 'rediscovery' of Christian worship—of that twofold 'service' to God and to the world which is expressed in the biblical term *leitourgia*—as the central and determinative act of the Church's life. There is no clearer evidence of

this than the joint theological work produced since the last Faith and Order Conference at Lund in 1952; the growth of the Liturgical Movement in virtually all Christian traditions; and the common recognition of an essential connection between the worship of the Church and its missionary task. It is heartening to realize that, at a time when Christians are perhaps more aware of the tragic estrangement of the world from the Church than ever before, God is so plainly calling us to rediscover together the joy, depth and power of Christian worship.

107. The time has come to give this rediscovery earnest attention throughout our churches. The study of worship has often been regarded as one of the 'compartments' of ecumenical conversation. It has often been controlled by theological assumptions not directly related to the actual worshipping life of the Church. But if theology is to reflect the whole faith of the Church, and if (as we believe) it is in *leitourgia* that the Church is to find the fulfilment of its life, then it is essential that we let that *leitourgia* speak for itself. It is of crucial importance that we should investigate its forms and structures, its language and spirit, in the expectation that this process may throw new light upon various theological positions and affirmations, perhaps even lend new meaning to them, and thus open new possibilities in ecumenical dialogue. Clearly this is one of the main tasks facing the churches in the coming decades.

108. Although it is not possible to enumerate the various dimensions of Christian worship which we have discussed and on which we have found ourselves in fundamental agreement, we do wish to register the following convictions:

(a) In Christian worship, God comes to us in Christ through the Holy Spirit, sustains us through his grace, establishes us in fellowship with him and with one another, and empowers us for his service in the world. In worship, we come to God in Christ, the True Worshipper, who by his incarnation, servanthood, obedience unto death, resurrection and ascension, has made us participants in the worship which he offers. In him, truly God, we have access to the Father; in him, truly Man, we are restored to our true nature as worshippers of God. Christian worship is, therefore, a service to God the Father by men redeemed by his Son, who are continually finding new life in the power of the Holy Spirit.

(b) Christian worship, as a participation in Christ's own self-offering, is an act formative of Christian community—an act, moreover, which is conducted within the context of the whole Church, and which represents the one, catholic Church. Ecclesiastical division among the churches, personal estrangement, and social division based upon class, race or nation contradict true worship, because they represent a failure fully to carry out the common ministry of reconciliation to which we are all called in Christ.

(*c*) Christian worship in the form of preaching is based upon the commandment of Jesus Christ and his promise that he himself will be present with the hearers, working in them by his word. In the whole of Christendom, concern about liturgy directly involves preaching based upon the Holy Scriptures. Accordingly the task of the preacher is to proclaim the prophetic and apostolic word, as set forth in the Scriptures of the Old and New Testaments, and to interpret this word of God's judgement and mercy in the contemporary situation.

(*d*) It is our participation in the worship of Christ's people through word and sacrament that makes possible our ministry in various kinds of worship in smaller groups and in individual devotion. The people of God, exercising this discipline of daily prayer and devotion, whether as individuals, families, or groups within the congregation, strengthens the worship of the whole congregation. Thus the public worship of the congregation and the private worship of individuals, families or groups are mutually dependent as necessary parts of the total ministry of Christ's people.

(*e*) Christian worship is the act by which the Church recognizes its identification with the whole creation and offers it to God in service. At the same time, it is an act in which all presumed self-sufficiency of this world is brought to an end, and all things are made new.

(*f*) Christian worship, set forth in Baptism and celebrated in the Eucharist, is grounded and centred in the historical ministry of Jesus Christ, his death and resurrection, and his exalted and continuing ministry. Such worship always includes the gathering of Christ's people, the preaching of the word of God, participation in Christ's self-offering and intercession for all men, and thanksgiving with joy.

(*g*) Christian worship is at once remembrance, communion and expectation. It points beyond the present moment to the tasks of Christian witness which lie before us, as we join in Christ's ministry to the world, and as we look to the consummation of God's kingdom; for this side of that kingdom all our doings in the Church are but partial anticipation of the glory which is to come.

109. Because of this consensus we heartily recommend to the churches for study the Report of the Theological Commission on Worship prepared for the Montreal Conference (*Faith and Order Findings*, Part III). We especially commend the theses on the meaning of Christian worship prepared by the European and East Asian Sections.[1]

[1] See *Faith and Order Findings*, Part III, pp. 16-22 and 31-3.

II. BAPTISM AND HOLY COMMUNION

110. We have also been aware of a growing consensus in regard to the two great acts of sacramental worship which find a place in most of our traditions, although we gladly acknowledge that some who do not observe these rites share in the spiritual experience of life in Christ.

Baptism:

111. The book *One Lord, One Baptism*[1] has clearly shown how wide is the agreement amongst the churches with regard to baptism. There attention is focused upon the baptism with which Jesus himself was baptized (Mark 10.38). This began with his acceptance of solidarity with sinners in his baptism in the Jordan and continued as he followed the path of the Suffering Servant through passion, death and resurrection. The Spirit that came upon Jesus comes also on the Church and unites his people with him in death and resurrection, in and through the baptismal action. Participation in Christ is the central meaning of baptism. Though disagreement remains between those who practise infant baptism and those who practise believer-baptism, all would insist that personal commitment is necessary for responsible membership in the body of Christ. For all, moreover, baptism is related not only to the individual but also to the Church, not only to momentary experience but to life-long growth of participation in Christ. Those who have been raised by the Holy Spirit to new life in Christ are led from baptism to confirmation (or its equivalent) and to Holy Communion. The life is necessarily one of continuing struggle but also of continuing experience of grace. In faith and obedience the baptized live for the sake of Christ, of his Church, and of the world which he loves.

112. We have found general agreement that the following elements should find a place within any comprehensive order of baptism:

(*a*) an acknowledgement of God's initiative in salvation, of his continuing faithfulness, and of our total dependence on his grace,

(*b*) a declaration of the forgiveness of sins in and through Christ,

(*c*) an invocation of the Holy Spirit,

(*d*) a renunciation of evil,

(*e*) a profession of faith in Christ,

(*f*) an affirmation that the person baptized is a child of God and is incorporated into the body of Christ, whereby he becomes a witness to the Gospel.

These will precede or follow baptism with water in the name of the Father and of the Son and of the Holy Spirit.

[1] SCM Press and Augsburg Publishing House, 1961; see pp. 45 ff.

113. We make some practical recommendations to the churches:

(*a*) Baptism is not solely a matter of individual concern, but is intimately connected with the corporate worship of the Church. It should normally be administered during a public service of worship, so that the members of the local congregation may be reminded of their own baptism, and may welcome into their fellowship those who are baptized and whom they are to nurture in the Christian faith.

(*b*) In order to make baptism more prominent in the life of the congregation, the sacrament might well be administered in public on great festival occasions, as was the practice of the Early Church. The use of Easter as one such occasion would emphasize the link between baptism and dying and rising with Christ.

114. Instruction in the meaning of baptism should be provided regularly and systematically for the whole worshipping community.

115. In addition to instruction in the theological meaning of baptism, the churches must always remind their members that this sacrament, which binds men to Christ in community, brings to an end all human estrangements in both Church and world based on differences of race or class.

Eucharist:

116. Baptism, once performed and never repeated, leads us into the continuous worshipping life of the 'royal priesthood' (I Peter 2.9), the people of God. In the Holy Eucharist or Lord's Supper, constantly repeated and always including both word and sacrament, we proclaim and celebrate a memorial of the saving acts of God (I Cor. 11.23-6). What God did in the incarnation, life, death, resurrection and ascension of Christ, he does not do again. The events are unique; they cannot be repeated or extended or continued. Yet in this memorial we do not only recall past events: God makes them present through the Holy Spirit who takes of the things of Christ and declares them to us, thus making us participants in Christ (I Cor. 1.9).

117. Despite many disagreements regarding Holy Communion and despite the desire of many for a fuller statement, we are drawn at least to agree that the Lord's Supper, a gift of God to his Church, is a sacrament of the presence of the crucified and glorified Christ until he come, and a means whereby the sacrifice of the cross, which we proclaim, is operative within the Church. In the Lord's Supper the members of the body of Christ are sustained in their unity with their Head and Saviour who offered himself on the cross: by him, with him and in him who is our great High Priest and Intercessor we offer to the Father, in the power of the Holy Spirit, our praise, thanksgiving and inter-

cession. With contrite hearts we offer ourselves as a living and holy
sacrifice, a sacrifice which must be expressed in the whole of our daily
lives. Thus united to our Lord, and to the Church triumphant, and in
fellowship with the whole Church on earth, we are renewed in the
covenant sealed by the blood of Christ. In the Supper we also anticipate
the marriage-supper of the Lamb in the Kingdom of God.

118. Orders of Holy Communion usually include the following
elements:

(a) A service of the word, containing:

   i. the reading and preaching of the word,
   ii. intercession for the whole Church and for the world.

(b) A service of the sacrament, having a shape determined by the
actions of our Lord at the Last Supper:

   i. taking bread and wine to be used by God in this service,
   ii. blessing God for creation and redemption and invoking the
Holy Spirit (or referring in some other way to the Holy Spirit);
reciting the words of institution, whether before or within or
after the prayer of thanksgiving; and saying the Lord's prayer,
   iii. breaking the bread,
   iv. giving the bread and the wine.

This list of liturgical items is not meant to exclude reference during the
service to many other important theological themes such as the expression of contrition; the declaration of forgiveness of sins; the affirmation
of faith in credal form; the celebration of the communion of saints; the
announcement of the Lord's coming; and the self-dedication of the
faithful to God. We assume that the person who presides will be someone recognized by his church as authorized to do so.

119. We are aware of certain practices which are being re-emphasized
by the Liturgical Movement, and we recommend to the churches that
they should seriously consider whether these might be even more
widely adopted:

(a) the frequent celebration of Holy Communion,
(b) the more active participation of the laity in the liturgy,
(c) the use of a common loaf of bread, and of a common cup,
(d) the reception of communion by the whole assembled congregation as the normal practice whenever the Eucharist is celebrated,
(e) the emphasis on the significance of Sunday and the great Christian
festivals.

120. We call attention to our recommendation for a new study of the
question of intercommunion, and register our approval of the principles
outlined therein for the regulation of services of Holy Communion at

ecumenical gatherings. The document produced by this Section is submitted through the Conference to the Central Committee of the W.C.C.[1]

III. CHRISTIAN WORSHIP IN THE WORLD TODAY

121. In her worship the Church rejoices that God is Lord of both the Church and the world. The Church is enjoined to be in the world but not of it. In worship Christians accept the world as the sphere of their obedience to God. They do so in the strength of their renewed life in Christ.

122. The worship of the churches is today celebrated within a world at once brilliant in technological achievement and deeply troubled. In both perennial and new forms, our world presents a face opposed or indifferent to Christian worship, or insensible to the good news of Christ. Sometimes heedless and apparently disdainful of any transcendent human destiny, men often affect a resolute endurance of meaninglessness when earthly preoccupations fade or measurable securities fail.

123. In the face of this situation, the worship of the churches warrants examination. The churches should ask themselves whether the liturgical language, images and symbols used are adequately intelligible to the modern mind. They might also inquire whether the language of the preached word helpfully illuminates the heritage of Christian faith in an idiom comprehensible to contemporary man. We suggest that it is the function of the Christian teacher to use with discrimination the language of the day to interpret what is enshrined in the liturgy. Although the liturgy employs the language of the Bible—a language associated with a world-view different from our own—the symbols and images of biblical language relate, not primarily to cosmology, but to man in his relations with God. Of these relations they remain authentic media; and sensitive preaching is required to recover the reality manifested in the symbols. The timely illumination of the biblical symbolism is part of the witness of the churches to modern man.

124. The churches should more fully consider how the use of art forms (music, painting, architecture, etc.) especially those which are contemporary, may make both their worship and their proclamation of the Gospel more meaningful for modern man. Special attention should be given to the ways in which architectural forms may assist, or obstruct, communication of the Faith.

IV. WORSHIP, MISSION AND INDIGENIZATION

125. We strongly commend to the thoughtful attention of the churches the searching discussion of worship and mission, and of

[1] For the full text of this document, as revised by the Central Committee of the W.C.C. at Rochester, U.S.A., in August 1963, see pp. 77 ff.

'indigenization', contained in the Report of the Theological Commission on Worship (*Faith and Order Findings*, Part III, pp. 37-40).

126. We heartily agree that mission is integral to worship. Thus we believe authentic Christian worship is both a witness to the world outside the Church, and also a renewed summons to believers within the Church 'to show forth the Lord's death till he comes'. We believe, further, that the Church's *leitourgia* in its wholeness is such a showing forth; for here we find a glad participation in the redemption in Christ, both in the worship of the sanctuary and in the common life of the world.

127. We find ourselves in strong agreement that the message of the Gospel must be enacted in a form, and proclaimed in an idiom, comprehensible by those to whom it is addressed. This enactment may be through the timely preaching of the word, through liturgy and rite, or through the 'living sacrifice' of Christian lives. Worship need not be unduly restricted to set forms or structures. When a man has a living faith in God, he should be encouraged to express it in spontaneous praise and thanksgiving.

128. Just as faith finds its own ways of expression in worship, so the Church's mission involves indigenization, a process of becoming rooted in the culture of the people. This process occurs normally, and most authentically, where Christian faith and worship possess the maturity and vitality to appropriate and convert prevailing cultural forms for the service of Christ. In this way Christian worship not only takes root in the culture but converts it to Christ, and so shares in the reconciliation of the whole creation to God. We ought not to be so much concerned with adapting worship to the local culture that we forget that the culture itself is to be transformed. Indigenization, we believe, is more nearly conversion than accommodation. The indigenization of Christian worship, required in every time and place, is the offering of the created order back to God, but converted and transfigured by the redemption that is in Christ.

COMMUNION SERVICES AT ECUMENICAL GATHERINGS

129. As already noted on p. 28, the Conference was under an obligation to send to the Central Committee of the W.C.C. some observations on this subject, and, if possible, certain recommendations which would advance beyond the point reached by the Lund Conference of 1952. The document which follows was originally prepared by the sub-section entitled 'Full Communion, Open Communion, Intercommunion'; was then discussed and approved by Section IV as a whole; was then discussed and approved by the Conference as a whole (a motion to delete Recommentation 3 being defeated by 118 votes to 51); and was finally discussed, slightly amended and approved

by the Central Committee of the W.C.C., meeting at Rochester, New York, U.S.A., in August 1963.

130. To avoid confusion it has been thought better to print only the final version as approved by the Rochester meeting, since it is in this standard form that it will reach the churches.

131. *Resolution:*

'The Central Committee, having received and noted the introduction and recommendations concerning Holy Communion at Ecumenical Gatherings sent to it by the Fourth World Conference on Faith and Order at Montreal, adopts the recommendations embodied in the following document and transmits the document as a whole to the member churches.'

132. The Fourth World Conference on Faith and Order noted the view of the New Delhi Assembly that a reconsideration is needed of the Lund recommendations regarding 'Communion Services at Ecumenical Gatherings' and agreed that this is demanded by the developments which have taken place since 1952 and the present situation within the World Council of Churches and the ecumenical movement in general.

133. There is deepened and deepening experience of unity among the churches committed to one another in the W.C.C. Indeed we believe that the reality, significance and implications of our *koinonia* within councils of churches in general and the W.C.C. in particular call urgently for further study. But it should be noted that, on the other hand, there has been an increase in the number of member churches which have difficulty in accepting intercommunion between separated churches as a satisfactory concept or procedure, while on the other hand there has appeared in certain quarters, and particularly among youth, though by no means confined to them, a growing impatience with certain of the traditional attitudes and hesitations on this matter.

134. It is much to be regretted that many churches do not yet appear to have responded to the request from Lund that they give attention to differences of eucharistic theology and practice, and to the new problems in this field arising from association in the World Council of Churches. Churches owe it to themselves to relate their theologies and their disciplines to the current situation.

135. Any substantial change from the intention behind the Lund recommendations would, we believe, be widely regarded as an ecumenical disaster with widespread and unfortunate consequences. It would be a betrayal of the deepening conviction of many in the W.C.C., and in national and local situations, that 'table fellowship' is demanded by 'Christian fellowship'. Moreover, whatever view is taken of intercommunion in general, the question arises whether ecumenical gatherings do not constitute a special case. In such gatherings we have to find

that arrangement of communion services which, while respecting the teaching of the churches and individual consciences, gives the fullest possible expression to the oneness of the Church of Christ which we all confess.

136. Each generation must inform itself about the differences there are in eucharistic theology and practice and of the changes that are taking place. The Faith and Order Commission might well in the years ahead devote to the sacrament of Holy Communion the attention recently devoted to baptism. Such attention would require document-ation of the eucharistic teaching and practice, including the liturgy, of the individual churches and would include careful study of recent suggestions for concelebration and an Agape-meal. We do not feel ready to express an opinion for or against either of these.[1]

137. The Report of the Commission on Intercommunion presented to the Lund Conference and commended by it to the churches for their study sets forth clearly the diversity of sacramental doctrine which prevents all the churches from favouring intercommunion. We believe that this report and the section on Intercommunion in the report of the Lund Conference are still worthy of attention. The con-tinuing diversity of views was again stated in the report of the Section on Unity of the New Delhi Assembly.

138. Some Christians believe that the degree of ecclesial communion which we have in the body of Christ, through baptism and through our fundamental faith, although we are still divided on some points, urges us to celebrate Holy Communion together and to promote inter-communion between the churches. It is Christ, present in the Eucharist, who invites all Christians to his table: this direct invitation of Christ cannot be thwarted by ecclesiastical discipline. In the communion at the same holy table, divided Christians are committed in a decisive way to make manifest their total, visible and organic unity.

139. Some Christians believe that eucharistic communion, being an expression of acceptance of the whole Christ, implies full unity in the wholeness of his truth; that there cannot be any 'intercommunion' between otherwise separated Christians; that communion in the sacraments therefore implies a pattern of doctrine and ministry, which is indivisible; and that 'intercommunion' cannot presume upon the union in faith that we still seek.

140. Between these two views of Holy Communion there are others, some approximating to one side, some to the other. But the sharp difference of conviction indicating two poles within the Council's membership must be recognized. However, as was said at the New

[1] To assist the study by the churches of the issues involved, they commend the paper on Intercommunion by Frère Max Thurian, and the questions addressed to the churches by the consultation held at Bossey in March 1961 (*Ecumenical Review*, vol. XIII, No. 3, April 1961).

Delhi Assembly, 'for neither view can there be any final peace so long as others who are known to be in Christ are not with us at the Holy Communion'.

141. Accordingly the Central Committee of the World Council of Churches agrees that the following procedures, subject to regular review, be applied to the Assembly and to other W.C.C. gatherings where it seems appropriate, and that they be recommended to the churches for their use as they may see fit. In doing so the Central Committee wishes to encourage the churches, when sending delegates to conferences, to inform them of these recommendations, and urge their delegates' cooperation where church discipline and individual conscience allow. It is assumed throughout that the responsibility for arranging the celebration of the Sacrament rests with the churches represented at such a conference and not with the W.C.C. itself.

142. It is recommended that:

(*a*) It be made clear in the printed programme that there are at present within the fellowship of the W.C.C. unresolved differences of eucharistic theology and practice.

(*b*) Arrangements be made within the programme of the conference for a Communion Service to be held at which an invitation to participate and partake is given to members of other churches. Such a service should if possible be at the invitation of one of the local churches (agreed upon after consultation with such of the locally represented churches as are in membership with the W.C.C.), or at the joint invitation of a number of such churches.

(*c*) Arrangements be made within the programme of the conference for one service of Holy Communion according to the liturgy of a church which cannot conscientiously offer an invitation to members of all other churches to partake of the elements. Such a service should be accompanied by an invitation to all the members to be present.

(*d*) There be in the programme a United Service of Preparation for Holy Communion at which emphasis shall be laid on (*a*) the divine mystery of salvation which the Lord's Supper proclaims, (*b*) our need for Christ and his forgiveness, (*c*) sorrow for the divisions of Christendom and for their continuance, (*d*) the unity in Christ given and experienced within the World Council of Churches, and (*e*) our responsibility to pray and work for a fuller manifestation of this unity.

(*e*) There be an opportunity outside the conference programme for Communion Services at such times as make it possible for every member of the conference to receive communion without violation of conscience or disloyalty to church tradition.

(*f*) It be recognized as fitting that arrangements be made for those whose normal practice is that of frequent or daily participation in Holy Communion. Such individuals should be invited to give special consideration to the attitude they should take to the Service proposed in paragraph (*b*), particularly when this is held on a Sunday.

(*g*) Where a conference is held in a place where there is only one member church and this church is unable to issue an open invitation, but is willing to arrange a celebration of the liturgy at which the members of the conference are invited to be present, such a liturgy be held on the first Sunday of the conference; but the conference authorities be empowered to make place in the programme for a service at which an invitation to participate and partake is given in accordance with paragraphs (*b*) and (*h*).

(*h*) Should an Assembly or other W.C.C. gathering be held in a place where no member church is represented locally, it should be regarded as appropriate that those responsible for the programme, after careful consultation with the churches sending delegates, invite one or more of those churches to make arrangements for services of Holy Communion in accordance with paragraphs (*b*) and (*c*).

Section V

' "ALL IN EACH PLACE": THE PROCESS OF GROWING TOGETHER'

INTRODUCTION

143. 'And they devoted themselves to the apostles' teaching and fellowship: to the breaking of bread and the prayers.' This description of the Church in the early chapters of Acts (see especially Acts 2.42 and 4.20) is particularly relevant to our present understanding of the local church. It is a gathering of believers in Jesus Christ under the leadership of the apostles, in a particular place, yet committed to a mission to the whole world.

144. In the course of Christian history, division and separation have taken place. Now, however, we live in an era when the churches are seeking to overcome their separations. The proving ground of unity is the local church. Here the process of growing together exhibits the fruits of the Spirit, the tensions of our divisions, and the strains and conflicts arising from the contemporary revolutionary situation. Here the divisive factors of racial enmity, class conflict and national and ideological loyalties, are acutely manifest in their relationship to Christian unity and mission.

145. Searching questions are raised as to whether the institutional patterns of our local churches and denominations are not increasingly obsolescent, in the light of our deepened understanding of the nature of the unity we seek, and because of the impact of secular challenges to our common calling. Our meeting together in the ecumenical movement compels us to face the division of the churches in each place. It is in the local community that the scandal of Christian disunity is particularly conspicuous and injurious. Therefore it is in each place where people live, work and worship, that our partnership in the body of Christ has to be made manifest and lived out. We gladly commend to the churches and denominational and ecumenical agencies for careful study the Report of the Study Commission on Institutionalism (*Faith and Order Findings*, Part I, pp. 3-29) and the accompanying symposium, *Institutionalism and Church Unity* (Association Press and SCM Press, 1963).

146. This Section report can deal only briefly with certain facets of the total complex of issues such as the relationship of the local church to the Church Universal; with some divisive factors such as those occasioned by race, class, and institutional structures; and with the demands of the mission of the Church in the local situation. We strongly urge local churches to commit themselves to ventures of obedience which make concrete the process of growing together in the Spirit. 'The universal must be local to be real.'

A. THE LOCAL CHURCH AND THE CHURCH UNIVERSAL:
BASIC THEOLOGICAL AFFIRMATIONS

I

147. In this report we refer to the body of Christ in all ages and all places as 'the Church Universal'. By 'the local congregation' we mean the local fellowship of Christians gathered for the hearing of the word and the celebration of the Lord's Supper according to Christ's ordinance. Each congregation is a manifestation of the Church Universal. We call attention to the statement in the Report of Section I (pp. 44 ff., paras. 24 and 26), 'Thus each . . . congregation participating in Christ is related to others not by participation in some higher structure or organization but rather by an identity of existence in Christ. . . . Some would hold that certain Christian communities claiming the name "church" do not fully manifest the one Church (and some too would add that no community fully manifests the one Church); but all would recognize that in these communities also Christ is present and his Lordship is acknowledged, and that their members in some sense therefore belong to the one Church.'

F

148. Other forms of church life may exist in a particular place, e.g.:

(a) groups established by the ministries of chaplains or by Christians from established congregations, such as 'house churches';

(b) groups arising in specific professions or trades, or in educational spheres;

(c) groups such as councils of churches.

149. Most of these groups bring together Christians of various denominations in a new ecumenical experience; some attach little significance to traditional allegiances and patterns of life; some represent fresh ways of Christian witness and fellowship which call seriously into question self-centred habits and established structures of church life.

150. The contemporary ecumenical situation presents us with the fact that both local congregations and these other forms of church life, taken together, constitute a new and complex manifestation of the Church. We shall refer to this manifestation as 'the local church'. This new situation imposes new obligations upon individual congregations and upon the whole company of Christians in each place.

151. These groups are significant for our understanding of the nature of the local church and for its renewal, because they show the ways in which Christians are trying in contemporary situations to express their fellowship in Christ and their obedience to him. These groups are to be encouraged, because they have freedom to experiment and can make relevant contributions to the renewal of the churches. Their nature as 'church' requires further study, however. Such groups must guard against becoming occasions of further division in the life of the one people of God, and should seek to maintain a vital relationship with the traditional centres of the Church's corporate life, worship and witness in each place.

152. We believe that the Church Universal is manifest in locality only as all Christians in that place fulfil the unity which is described in the statement of the New Delhi Assembly of the World Council of Churches (cp. *New Delhi Speaks*, SCM Press, 1962, p. 55):

'We believe that the unity which is both God's will and his gift to his Church is being made visible as all in each place who are baptized into Jesus Christ and confess him as Lord and Saviour are brought by the Holy Spirit into one fully committed fellowship, holding the one apostolic faith, preaching the one Gospel, breaking the one bread, joining in common prayer, and having a corporate life reaching out in witness and service to all, and who at the same time are united with the whole Christian fellowship in all places and all ages in such wise that ministry and members are accepted by all, and that all can act and speak together as occasion requires for the tasks to which God calls his people.'

II

153. Members of local churches belong together despite their separation into different congregations. Through worship and sacraments, faith and doctrine, witness and service, they share in the treasures of the whole Church. However, being separated, they are deprived of full participation in these things, and must make bold ventures in ecumenical obedience together.

Worship and Sacraments

154. Through baptism and faith, Christians are brought into the life of the Church Universal as well as into the visible community of the local church. Our common baptism is thus a basic bond of unity by which we are called as one people to confess and serve one Lord in each place and in all the world.[1] Worship, as the act of the Church in which the one God and Father of all is glorified and his word in the Bible communicated, similarly expresses and strengthens participation in the wholeness of the Church. Thus the congregation does not worship by itself; it worships in and with the whole Church as the communion of saints. Because Christ himself is present in our acts of worship, these acts at the same time express and strengthen our communion with him and with one another, although they are still performed in our divided traditions. Holy Communion is also the act of the Church in which the churches break the one bread with the Lord himself present. Thus in spite of our painful separation at the Lord's Table we have communion in him who gives himself in every act of communion. Here too, in ecumenical obedience, the local church is called to make manifest in itself the presence of the one Church.

155. This understanding of worship and sacraments lays upon us a strong obligation to pray and work constantly for the day when all Christians in each place can come together freely in common worship and at the Lord's Table.

Faith and Doctrine

156. The treasure of traditions and experience, of knowledge and insight, which have been given to the whole Church, are available to the local church. A congregation cannot effectively witness amid contemporary challenges and confusions unless it is always striving in faith and obedience to enter into the wholeness of the truth which the Church everywhere proclaims. In this activity the congregation is both corrected and enriched, and may also make its contribution to the

---

[1] It is recognized that the Friends and the Salvation Army, while not using the visible forms of baptism and the Lord's Supper, share in the common response of faith to the word of God.

understanding of Christian truth by its own fresh insights and experiences.

157. The growing ecumenical fellowship is making the riches of common Christian truth more easily available to all Christians, and this too places upon us the obligation to share more fully in the life of the whole Church.

Witness and Service

158. The Faith and Order Conference at Lund, 1952, enunciated the principle that churches should act together in all matters except those in which deep differences of conviction compelled them to act separately. Those accepting this principle have discovered thereby a richer quality of life and an experience of participating in the whole Church. Local congregations have come to this experience by sharing in World Council of Churches' projects, and by seeking to fulfil together other Christian obligations in society. This justifies the claim that Christian service can be an experience through which the local church realizes that it is the Church Universal in a particular place.

159. Yet many congregations are still not sharing in such enterprises; consequently they are not assuming their real place. Furthermore, the present cooperative activities possess only a limited significance; when they give place to fully united forms of service, all local churches will experience more adequately the life of the whole Church.

160. In the modes of Christian activity mentioned above, therefore, we see experiences in which the nature of the Church, as universal and as local, is manifest. We would urge local churches to accept more fully the obligation involved in this truth and thus to experience in fresh ways the life of the Church Universal.

III

161. A word must also be written about the place of the denomination in the life of the Church. In the New Testament the word '*ekklesia*' is used only of local congregations and of the universal Church. Apostolic writings emphasize the unity of all believers in Christ. Today, however, we use the word 'church' to denote denominations which are neither merely local nor fully universal.

162. The ecclesiological significance of denominations is by no means clear; it needs full and careful examination. Here we can make only three comments:

   (*a*) Denominations have been instrumental in developing fresh insights into Christian truth with new modes of worship, fellowship and service; in providing local churches with experiences of wider community; in maintaining within them proper order and genuine stability; and in offering an enriching diversity.

(b) Yet the denominational system cannot be regarded as an essential form of church life, in the same way in which the congregation is essential.

(c) At times denominations have caused rivalries among local congregations and have expressed and consolidated divisions among Christians. Denominational fragmentation, which in some areas of the world exists in extreme forms, distorts the true nature of the Church and obstructs the communication of the Gospel. It is not sufficient simply to refer to these facts as the sinful elements in denominational divisions; they raise inescapable questions about the structures themselves and suggest their provisional character.

B. THE CHURCH'S INVOLVEMENT IN A DIVIDED SOCIETY

163. The one Church is not only rent in its life and witness by internal divisions. It is also deeply involved in the conflicts and divisions of the world; and it all too often denies in its own fellowship that ministry of reconciliation which it is called to exercise among all men.

I

164. The very first question that man addresses to God in the Bible is that of his responsibility towards his brother: 'Am I my brother's keeper?' (Gen. 4.9). The question underlines man's basic propensity to set his hand against his fellows and to deny the fundamental solidarity of all mankind under God. Man is rooted in enmity, contradiction, apathy, estrangement and sin. But this very man was reconciled to God and to his fellow man in Jesus Christ—once and for all time. It is this same Christ in whom the Church lives today.

165. God does not ask the sex of a person, or the colour of his skin, or his social class, or the economic status he holds, or his language, or his political affiliation, or his denomination, before he acknowledges that same man as his own creature and his child, and calls him to eternal life.

166. But does the life of the Church in each place assert the dignity of the human person as God's gift? Do we believe that every Christian in every place must selflessly witness to the fact that God is no respecter of labels, and that all men everywhere are of one blood under him?

II

167. We are shamefully divided by racial prejudice and discrimination. This denies the dignity of man, subverts our unity in Christ, and

stultifies the mission of the Church. God is judging our racially divided Christian communities through the contemporary revolutionary events in many parts of the world. In Christ there is no defence or excuse for the wilful continuation of groups, church meetings or fellowships which are racially exclusive. We therefore call upon Christians in their local churches to show the marks of Christian discipleship whatever the cost.

168. We are also divided by ethnic, cultural and tribal loyalties. We recognize that, in the providence of God, human life is sustained by communities of language, custom and culture. The churches have properly ministered to their people in and through their varieties of tongues, customs and art forms. Indeed cultural unities have sometimes nourished Christian unity. But these divisions of the human family too often mask our oneness in Christ, and are maintained with a passion that makes them idols. The ethnic, cultural and tribal divisions between and within congregations in each place call all Christians to self-examination and repentance.

169. The Christian community is often divided by rigid denominationalism. While we rejoice that there are some signs of cooperation for the witness to the unity of the Church in some areas, in many places churches with common confessions of faith still remain denominationally separated, long after any defence of such separation can be made in the light of the Gospel. Institutional self-interest often maintains division in local churches to the detriment of the mission of the Church. The churches are called to overcome inertia and denominational pride, which alienate believer from believer and hinder the proclamation of oneness in Christ.

170. Identification with a particular social class; preference for a particular style of life; commitment to a political philosophy or party; achievement in economic life and education, etc.—these also often threaten the wholeness of the Christian community in each place. In themselves, these factors represent a social diversity which often serves human good. Yet the same loyalties must not be allowed to supplant the loyalty of a congregation to its one Lord.

III

171. Christians are today being brought together by the mobility of people, by migration, by nation-building, by the struggle for human freedom and justice, and even by the social and political oppression of the Church. Christians (both as individuals and as a body) are often passive recipients rather than active participants in processes which can enhance human and Christian community. With opportunities such as these which are made possible by God, there is also given a

command to form local Christian communities that witness visibly to our oneness in creation and redemption.

172. This command entails study and action. Congregations, councils, and church leaders in various regions and social conditions, should bring disciplined analysis to bear on what divides and what unites Christians in each place. The varieties of place—metropolitan areas and declining villages, new nations and old empires, tribal pluralism and racial diversity, etc.—require local study. The resources not only of theology and ethics, but also of social and behavioural sciences, need to be used to understand why all are not together in each place, and to break down the walls of division.

173. Unity is the fruit of Christian discipleship, and the latter takes various forms. A common protest against unjust laws which create or enforce racial divisions will make clearer the oneness in Christ. Crossing social barriers for Bible study and prayer, for labour and recreation, can bring new forms and levels of unity into existence. Cooperative activities in ministry and fellowship, when done even in advance of consensus within a denomination or of the strict interpretation of canon law, can promote unity. Mutual visitation and personal contact can break new ground. Participation in the worship of God through unfamiliar cultural idioms and expressions may lead to new experiences of all being one in a given place.

174. There are circumstances in which witness to unity, however simple, is costly. Yet the cross is the measure of discipleship. Whatever the circumstances, Christians can and should witness to unity, and accept responsibility for their brothers.

C. THE MISSION OF THE PEOPLE OF GOD IN EACH PLACE

I

175. If the unity which is 'God's will and his gift to his Church' is to be made visible, it is essential that local churches accept the missionary obligation which God has given to his whole Church. More insistently and urgently than for centuries, we are being asked: 'Are you really sharing the life that is in Jesus Christ, because to share in it is to take part in his mission to the world?'

176. It is only as all in each place respond to this call to be God's people in and for their particular 'world', as well as in and for the whole world, that they will enter into the unity of one committed fellowship.

II

177. If we accept this responsibility, searching and uncomfortable questions are raised about our present situation as churches in country

area, town, city, state or nation, whether we are congregations of one denomination or of several.

178. *As Christians forming a local congregation,*

Do we know ourselves to be the body of which Christ is the Head, and do we know

that we have been given a message we need not be afraid or ashamed to proclaim;

that we are called to accept the cost as well as the joy of discipleship;

and that in the world where we are his people, he is also Lord, no matter where or in what circumstances we live?

Is his lordship the power as well as the consolation in our lives as individuals and in the fellowship?

Is our offering of worship something confined to certain times and buildings, or is it the total and thankful giving of ourselves to Christ and to all in need?

Are the inherited patterns and rhythms of our congregational life now at many points outmoded and unsuited to the proper functioning of the Church in its contemporary mission?

179. *As Christians in relation to neighbouring congregations*

Do we think of ourselves as bound together in the mission laid on us all in each place, or does the recognition of other churches in the same locality as ourselves evoke merely a general sentiment of goodwill?

Is Christ really our one Head, so that we must seek together to know his commands and to do them?

Do we see the significance of the fact that as we go out into the world in service and witness, we meet one another there in our common tasks and mission, face the same problems of allegiance, and rely alike on the one Holy Spirit?

180. *As Christians in the world,*

Are we manifestly a community in which men and women are being made new in Christ, are caught up into a purpose greater than themselves, and identify themselves with the oppressed, the downtrodden, and the victims of injustice, misfortune, prejudice or greed? Does our ministry of reconciliation include also those who cause oppression and injustice?

Is God's reconciling grace seen in our midst breaking down every wall of separation in race, colour, caste, tribe, sex, class or nation—or do we present to the world a spectacle of disunity at a time when the world itself is creating its own unities and seeking still deeper unity?

181. In our local situations we often find ourselves the inheritors of traditions which, though we gratefully acknowledge that it was in them that we came to know God in Christ, separate us from our brethren who share the same faith and are committed to the same allegiance as ourselves. If we have absolutized the channels through which the truth of God in Christ has come to us, we must turn again in repentance, through him who is himself the Truth, and accept one another.

III

182. Adequate answers to these questions will be found only as 'all in each place' seek them together. We have no blueprint to offer that will cover the variety of local situations. Nevertheless, we are convinced that the Spirit is pointing us toward some quite definite ways where obedience and action are required of us, and we wish to commend these to our brethren in local churches.

183. The first step is the serious recognition that through baptism we are one people serving the one Lord in each place.

184. Even in our present separation as churches, this provides the basis for 'joint action for mission'—i.e. the application of the total resources of all churches in one place to mission in that place and in the world at large.

185. The actual pattern of this growing partnership can, and should, be infinitely varied and flexible. But two principles will govern it:

(a) It will be directed to the 'normal' life of local congregations and not to some optional area of 'ecumenical cooperation'.

(b) It will demand a willingness to accept responsible risks in relation to traditional patterns of church life (congregational, denominational or confessional), in which both local congregations and denominational authorities must share.

186. In some areas, for instance, a pattern of joint action is emerging at three levels:

(a) a council of churches covering the whole area;

(b) a close partnership of congregations within each immediate neighbourhood;

(c) various groupings of Christians of different denominations and confessions in the places where they live and work.

187. Whatever the pattern, joint action for mission will involve the churches in the following:

(a) *surveying* together, through their most representative and responsible leadership, the total mission confronting the churches, especially in the significant areas of industry, the student world,

politics, the professions, and in areas of human need in the modern
state;

(*b*) *recognizing* that the whole people of God, clergy and laity, are
alike committed to sharing in Christ's ministry in the world;

(*c*) *realizing* that problems facing laymen in the world today have
no denominational answers;

(*d*) *acting* together for the training of the laity for their ministry in
the world, and making full use of the insights and experiences of
laymen in their daily work;

(*e*) *experimenting* in joint training of candidates for baptism, confirmation or full church membership, towards a common understanding of their one faith and calling.

188. A fully effective 'lay apostolate' can be properly trained for
mission and ministry in the world only as it is representative of *all* in
each place.

D. CONCLUSION

189. We are conscious of being heirs of the manifold riches of God's
grace in Christ.

190. We acknowledge that many of God's gifts to his whole Church
cannot be shared by us in our local churches until we recognize ourselves as the one people of God in each place, and are prepared to
embody this fact in new and bold ventures of living faith today.

191. Such joint action as we have commended to the churches in this
report calls for repentance, that we do not yet adequately bear witness
to the fact that we are the one people of God. It calls for a serious
examination of our confesssional, denominational and congregational
structures to see how far they support or hinder our growing together
as God's one people. It calls also for a serious study of what constitutes
the ecumenical training of the ministry, especially those who will
serve the churches in local ministries.

192. Above all, it calls us in the Church everywhere to ask unceasingly
for the Spirit that renews, empowers, unites and commits us joyfully,
and at whatever cost, to God's mission in each place and in all the
world. The process of growing together into that unity which God
wills for his Church is even now opening up with new and exciting
possibilities.

So we pray: Come, Holy Spirit.

4

LIST OF CONFERENCE OFFICERS

Conference Chairman: The Rt Rev. O. S. Tomkins, Bishop of Bristol.

Conference Vice-Chairmen: The Most Rev. Chrysostomos, Metropolitan of Myra; Professor H. D'Espine; Professor A. C. Outler.

Chairman of Business Committee: Dr D. Horton.

Chairman of Worship Committee: Professor J. R. Nelson.

Chairman of Press Committee: Principal G. Johnston.

(For Section officers, see Section lists.)

5

MEMBERS OF THE SECTIONS

Section I: 'The Church in the Purpose of God'

Name	Country	Church
Professor J. M. Aagaard	Denmark	Church of Denmark (Lutheran)
The Rev. J. M. Bates	New Zealand	Presbyterian Church of New Zealand
Dr G. R. Beasley-Murray (*Bible Study Leader*)	U.K.	Baptist Union of Gt Britain and Ireland
The Rev. V. Berzonsky	U.S.A.	Russian Orthodox Greek Catholic Church of North America
Dr R. S. Bilheimer	U.S.A.	United Presbyterian Church (U.S.A.)
Professor A. J. Bronkhorst	Belgium	Netherlands Reformed Church
The Rev. R. E. Brown	U.S.A.	Roman Catholic Church
The Rev. A. Brunet	Canada	Roman Catholic Church
Mr A. Buevsky	U.S.S.R.	Orthodox Church of Russia
Dr W. K. Clymer	U.S.A.	Evangelical United Brethren Church
Professor V. W. Couillard	U.S.A.	Moravian Church in America (Northern Province)
Professor G. R. Cragg (*Chairman*)	U.S.A.	United Church of Canada
Mr G. Cram	Canada	United Church of Canada
Dr P. A. Crow, Jr	U.S.A.	Disciples of Christ (U.S.A.)
Metropolitan Cyprian of Monemvasias and Spartis	Greece	Church of Greece (Orthodox)
Metropolitan Damascenos of Demetriados	Greece	Church of Greece (Orthodox)
Professor W. Dantine	Austria	Evangelical Church of Augsburg and Helvetic Confession (Austria)
The Rt Rev. A. Dun	U.S.A.	Protestant Episcopal Church (U.S.A.)
Professor G. A. Dunger	U.S.A.	North American Baptist General Conference
The Rev. B. Ederma	Canada	Estonian Evangelical Lutheran Church in Exile
Professor W. O. Fennell	Canada	United Church of Canada
Professor G. Florovsky (*Vice-Chairman*)	U.S.A.	Greek Orthodox Archdiocese of N. and S. America, Ecumenical Patriarchate
Mr D. Freiday	U.S.A.	Religious Society of Friends: Friends General Conference

Dr W. J. Gallagher	Canada	United Church of Canada
Dr D. Gelzer	Cameroun	Presbyterian Church of Cameroun
Professor J. L. Gonzalez	Puerto Rico	Methodist Church (U.S.A.)
Mr D. Grayston	Canada	Anglican Church of Canada
Professor W. F. Groff	U.S.A.	Church of the Brethren
Dr J. C. Groot	Netherlands	Roman Catholic Church
The Rev. M. B. Handspicker	U.S.A.	United Church of Christ (U.S.A.)
Professor J. W. Heikkinen	U.S.A.	Lutheran Church in America
Dr D. Horton	U.S.A.	United Church of Christ (U.S.A.)
Metropolitan Iakovos of Elassonos	Greece	Church of Greece (Orthodox)
The Rt Rev. T. G. V. Inman, Bishop of Natal	South Africa	Church of the Province of South Africa (Anglican)
Archbishop John	U.S.A.	Orthodox Church of Russia
The Rev. K. M. John	India	Church of South India
Dr J. A. Johnson	U.S.A.	Christian Methodist Episcopal Church
Professor P. de Jong	Canada	United Church of Canada
Dr R. Jungkuntz	U.S.A.	Lutheran Church—Missouri Synod
Professor E. Käsemann	Germany	Evangelical Church in Germany
Dr C. Kishi	Japan	Japan Evangelical Lutheran Church
Dr F. H. Klooster	U.S.A.	Christian Reformed Church
Dr K. S. Knutson	U.S.A.	The American Lutheran Church
Mr F. Kokuma	Ghana	Evangelical Presbyterian Church of Ghana
Professor G. W. H. Lampe (*Vice-Chairman*)	U.K.	Church of England
The Rev. W. A. Landman	South Africa	Dutch Reformed Church in South Africa
Professor W. H. Lazareth	U.S.A.	Lutheran Church in America
The Rt Rev. T. Mar Athanasius	India	Mar Thoma Syrian Church of Malabar
Professor P. S. Minear	U.S.A.	United Church of Christ (U.S.A.)
Professor D. Moody	U.S.A.	Southern Baptist Convention
The Very Rev. D. F. Najdanovich	Canada	Serbian Orthodox Church
The Ven. R. K. Naylor	Canada	Anglican Church of Canada
Professor J. R. Nelson	U.S.A.	The Methodist Church (U.S.A.)
Dr E. Newberry	U.S.A.	Church of God, Anderson, Indiana
Professor W. Niesel	Germany	Evangelical Church in Germany (R)
Dr S. F. Nishi	U.S.A.	Protestant Episcopal Church (U.S.A.)
The Rev. W. A. Norgren	U.S.A.	Protestant Episcopal Church (U.S.A.)
Bishop A. Nygren	Sweden	Church of Sweden
Professor J. A. Oosterbaan	Netherlands	General Mennonite Society
The Rev. A. M. van Peski	Netherlands	Remonstrant Brotherhood, Netherlands

The Rev. B. Probowinoto	Indonesia	Christian Churches in Mid-Java
Dr J. Radha Krishan	India	The Methodist Church (U.S.A.)
Professor J. S. Romanides	U.S.A.	Greek Orthodox Archdiocese of N. and S. America, Ecumenical Patriarchate
Mr J. M. Ross	U.K.	Presbyterian Church of England
The Rev A. Sapsezian	Brazil	Armenian Evangelical Church (Brazil)
Professor E. Schweizer (*Secretary*)	Switzerland	Swiss Protestant Church Federation
Professor J. E. Skoglund (*Secretary*)	U.S.A.	American Baptist Convention
Dr R. Slenczka	Germany	Evangelical Church in Germany (L)
Professor J. Smolik	Czechoslovakia	Evangelical Church of Czech Brethren
Dr H. H. Straton	U.S.A.	American Baptist Convention
The Rev. D. S. Sumbwana-yambe	N. Rhodesia	United Church of Central Africa
Archpriest I. W. Susemihl	U.S.S.R.	Orthodox Church of Russia
Dr G. A. Thiele	U.S.A.	Lutheran Church—Missouri Synod
Archbishop Tiran	U.S.A.	Armenian Apostolic Church
The Rt Rev. B. N. Y. Vaughan, Bishop of Mandeville	Jamaica	Church of the Province of the West Indies (Anglican)
Professor C. K. Von Euw	U.S.A.	Roman Catholic Church
Dr W. J. Villaume	Canada	Lutheran Church in America
Professor C. Welch	U.S.A.	The Methodist Church (U.S.A.)
The Rt Rev. G. O. Williams, Bishop of Bangor	U.K.	Church in Wales (Anglican)
Professor J. W. Winterhager	Germany	Evangelical Church in Germany (U)
Professor H. H. Wolf	Germany	Evangelical Church in Germany (L)
Professor H. F. Woodhouse	Ireland	Church of Ireland
The Rev. J. T. Yashiro	Japan	Anglican Church in Japan

Section II: 'Scripture, Tradition and Traditions'

Professor S. E. Ahlstrom	U.S.A.	Lutheran Church in America
The Rev. A. M. Allchin	U.K.	Church of England
Professor E. J. F. Arndt	U.S.A.	United Church of Christ (U.S.A.)
Metropolitan Athenagoras of Elaia	Canada	Greek Orthodox Archdiocese of N. and S. America, Ecumenical Patriarchate
Archbishop Basile	Belgium	Orthodox Church of Russia
The Rev. G. G. Beazley, Jr.	U.S.A.	Disciples of Christ (U.S.A.)
Professor A. Benoît	France	Evangelical Church of Augsburg Confession in Alsace and Lorraine

Professor C. J. I. Bergendoff	U.S.A.	Lutheran Church in America
Professor P. M. Bretscher	U.S.A.	Lutheran Church—Missouri Synod
The Rev. S. K. Bunker	Ceylon	Church of South India
Dr R. C. Chalmers	Canada	United Church of Canada
Metropolitan Chrysostomos of Myra	Turkey	Ecumenical Patriarchate of Constantinople
The Rev. P. D. Clasper	Burma	Burma Baptist Convention
Dr M. C. Crouse	U.S.A.	The Advent Christian General Conference of America
Dr M. E. Culver	U.S.A.	The Methodist Church (U.S.A.)
Professor H. D'Espine	Switzerland	Swiss Protestant Church Federation
Dr V. E. Devadutt	U.S.A.	American Baptist Convention
Professor E. Dinkler	Germany	Evangelical Church in Germany (U)
Professor M. Doi	Japan	United Church of Christ in Japan
The Rev. J. Drew	U.S.A.	Roman Catholic Church
Professor E. R. Fairweather	Canada	Anglican Church of Canada
Dr J. E. Farup	South Africa	Evangelical Lutheran Church in Southern Africa— South-East Region
Dr E. Flesseman-van Leer	Netherlands	Netherlands Reformed Church
The Rev. D. S. Green	U.S.A.	The Methodist Church (U.S.A.)
Professor S. L. Greenslade (*Vice-Chairman*)	U.K.	Church of England
The Rev. H.-C. Hahn	Germany	Moravian Church in Germany
The Rev. V. E. W. Hayward	U.K.	Baptist Union of Gt Britain and Ireland
Rabbi P. Hiat	U.S.A.	Synagogue Council of America
Dr R. Holte	Sweden	Church of Sweden
Dr W. M. Horton	U.S.A.	United Church of Christ (U.S.A.)
Dr L. Hunt	Canada	Anglican Church of Canada
The Rev. L. F. Hurley	U.S.A.	Seventh Day Baptist General Conference
Dr C. H. Hwang (*Bible Study Leader*)	Taiwan	Presbyterian Church in Formosa
Professor C. F. Johnston	Canada	United Church of Canada
Lt-Col P. S. Kaiser	U.S.A.	Salvation Army
The Rev. N. Karjomaa	Finland	Orthodox Church in Finland (Ecumenical Patriarchate)
Professor F. W. Kantzen- bach	Germany	Evangelical Church in Ger- many (L)
Dr J. Knudsen	U.S.A.	Lutheran Church in America
Professor W. F. A. Küppers	Germany	Old Catholic Church in Germany
The Rev. M.-A. Ledoux	New Caledonia	Evangelical Church in New Caledonia and the Loyalty Isles
Professor J.-L. Leuba	Switzerland	Swiss Protestant Church Federation
Dr U. S. Leupold	Canada	Lutheran Church in America
Professor G. A. Lindbeck	U.S.A.	Lutheran Church in America

The Rev. H. W. Lowe	U.S.A.	General Conference of Seventh Day Adventists
The Rev. S. Macdonnell	Canada	Presbyterian Church in Canada
Dr J. J. Markarian	Lebanon	Union of Armenian Evangelical Churches in the Near East
The Rev. J. Martucci	Canada	Roman Catholic Church
Professor D. M. Mathers	Canada	United Church of Canada
The Rev. R. E. Maxwell	U.S.A.	Protestant Episcopal Church (U.S.A.)
Professor G. Mayeda	Japan	Mukyokai (Non-Church Movement)
Professor R. Mehl	France	Reformed Church of Alsace and Lorraine
Metropolitan Meliton of Heliopolis	Turkey	Ecumenical Patriarchate of Constantinople
The Rt Rev. D. R. Miller	Jamaica	Presbyterian Church of Jamaica
Professor E. Molland (*Chairman*)	Norway	Church of Norway
Professor J. Moltmann	Germany	Evangelical Church in Germany (R)
Principal K. L. Nasir	Pakistan	United Presbyterian Church of Pakistan
The Rev. R. A. Nelson (*Vice-Chairman*)	Ireland	Methodist Church in Ireland
Dr J. Newton	U.K.	Methodist Church in Gt Britain
The Rev. N. Nicolaescu	Rumania	Rumanian Orthodox Church
Dr N. A. Nissiotis	Greece	Church of Greece (Orthodox)
Dr H. J. Ockenga	U.S.A.	Congregational
The Rev. D. J. O'Hanlon	U.S.A.	Roman Catholic Church
The Rev. D. Pourchot	Canada	Lutheran Church—Missouri Synod
Dr W. A. Quanbeck	U.S.A.	The American Lutheran Church
Dr B. L. Ramm	U.S.A.	American Baptist Convention
The Rev. E. C. Reckard	U.S.A.	United Presbyterian Church (U.S.A.)
Professor J. K. S. Reid (*Secretary*)	U.K.	Church of Scotland (Presbyterian)
Dr H. Reiss	Germany	Evangelical Church in Germany (U)
Professor V. C. Samuel	India	Orthodox Syrian Church of the East
Dean K. V. Sarkissian (*Secretary*)	Lebanon	Armenian Apostolic Church
The Rev. L. P. Schroeder	New Zealand	Methodist Church of New Zealand
The Rev. J. F. Seunarine	Trinidad	Presbyterian Church in Trinidad and Grenada
The Rt Rev. P. L. Simoes	Brazil	Brazilian Episcopal Church (Protestant Episcopal Church, U.S.A.)
The Rev. G. G. Smith	N. Rhodesia	United Church of Central Africa
Dr J. W. V. Smith	U.S.A.	Church of God, Anderson, Indiana

Professor N. H. Söe	Denmark	Church of Denmark
The Rev. G. Tavard	U.S.A.	Roman Catholic Church
Dr T. M. Taylor	U.S.A.	United Presbyterian Church (U.S.A.)
Dr S. A. Teinonen	Finland	Evangelical Lutheran Church of Finland
Dr J. N. Thomas	U.S.A.	Presbyterian Church in the United States
Dr R. Tobias	U.S.A.	——
Dr F. W. Tomkins	U.S.A.	Protestant Episcopal Church (U.S.A.)
Dr L. Vischer	Switzerland	Swiss Protestant Church Federation
Archpriest L. Voronov	U.S.S.R.	Orthodox Church of Russia
Canon H. M. Waddams	U.K.	Church of England
Professor H. H. Walsh	Canada	Anglican Church of Canada
Mr D'A. Wood	Australia	Methodist Church of Australasia
Dr J. H. Yoder	U.S.A.	General Conference Mennonite Church

SECTION III: 'The Redemptive Work of Christ and the Ministry of his Church'

The Rt Rev. C. W. Alderson, Bishop of Mashonaland	S. Rhodesia	Church of the Province of Central Africa (Anglican)
Professor R. F. Aldwinckle	Canada	Baptist Federation of Canada
Professor J.-J. von Allmen	Switzerland	Swiss Protestant Church Federation
The Rev. W. Artus	Uruguay	Waldensian Church of Rio de la Plata
The Rev. G. Baum	Canada	Roman Catholic Church
Professor H. Beintker	Germany	Evangelical Church in Germany (L)
Dr E. C. Blake	U.S.A.	United Presbyterian Church (U.S.A.)
Professor J. Bosc (*Bible Study Leader*)	France	Reformed Church of France
Dr K. R. Bowes	Australia	Federal Conference of the Churches of Christ in Australia
Mrs Porter Brown	U.S.A.	The Methodist Church (U.S.A.)
Dr R. H. Bullock	U.S.A.	Presbyterian Church in the United States
Mr F. Caloren	Canada	Presbyterian Church in Canada
Professor N. Chitescu	Rumania	Rumanian Orthodox Church
The Rev. W. H. Clark	U.S.A.	Protestant Episcopal Church (U.S.A.)
Dean J. B. Coburn (*Vice-Chairman*)	U.S.A.	Protestant Episcopal Church (U.S.A.)
The Rev. S. B. Coles	Canada	Presbyterian Church in Canada

G

The Rev. G. C. Dalzell	Canada	Presbyterian Church in Canada
The Rev. R. E. Davies	U.K.	Methodist Church in Gt Britain
The Rev. H. M. De Wolfe	Canada	Baptist Federation of Canada
Dr A. E. Fernandez Arlt	Uruguay	Lutheran Church in Uruguay
Dr F. V. Filson	U.S.A.	United Presbyterian Church (U.S.A.)
Dr H. Flottorp	Norway	Church of Norway
Bishop O. G. Fonceca	Philippines	United Church of Christ in the Philippines
Dr I. M. Fraser	U.K.	Church of Scotland
Dr A. A. Fulton	U.K.	Presbyterian Church in Ireland
Mr M. J. Gudgeon	U.K.	Church of England
Professor E. Guerra	Mexico	Congregational Church of Mexico
The Rev. E. E. Hallman	Canada	Evangelical United Brethren Church
Dr C. F. H. Henry	U.S.A.	American Baptist Convention
Commissioner S. Hepburn	U.S.A.	Salvation Army
Miss K. B. Hockin	Canada	United Church of Canada
The Rt Rev. A. M. Hollis	U.K.	Church of England
The Rev. J. R. Hord	Canada	United Church of Canada
Miss R. C. Howard	U.K.	Church of England
Professor R. D. Hyslop	U.S.A.	United Church of Christ (U.S.A.)
Professor W. Joest	Germany	Evangelical Church in Germany (L)
Dr R. C. Johnson	U.S.A.	United Presbyterian Church (U.S.A.)
Metropolitan Justin of Moldavia	Rumania	Rumanian Orthodox Church
Dr C. C. Kim	Korea	Presbyterian Church in the Republic of Korea
The Rev. P. L. Kjeseth	U.S.A.	The American Lutheran Church
The Rev. J. Kleeman	Germany	Evangelical Church in Germany
Professor G. Konidaris	Greece	Church of Greece (Orthodox)
The Rev. G. Langevin	Canada	Roman Catholic Church
Dr T. A. Langford	U.S.A.	The Methodist Church (U.S.A.)
The Rev. J.-M. Langlais	Canada	Roman Catholic Church
Dr J. Larson	U.S.A.	United Presbyterian Church (U.S.A.)
The Rev. J. P. Lee-Woolf	U.K.	Congregational Union of England and Wales
Mr P. P. van Lelyveld	Netherlands	Netherlands Reformed Church
Dr B. Lesko (*Vice-Chairman*)	Argentina	United Evangelical Lutheran Church of Argentina
Professor J. D. McCaughey (*Chairman*)	Australia	Presbyterian Church of Australia
Dr G. O. McCulloh	U.S.A.	The Methodist Church (U.S.A.)
Dr A. B. McDiarmid	New Zealand	Associated Churches of Christ in New Zealand
Miss F. Maeda	U.S.A.	United Presbyterian Church (U.S.A.)

Canon J. Maung Pe	Burma	Church of India, Pakistan, Burma and Ceylon (Anglican)
The Rev. L. P. Meyer	U.S.A.	Church of God, Anderson, Indiana
Dr J. Michalko	Czechoslovakia	Evangelical Church in Slovakia, Augsburg Confession
Lt-Col. F. Moulton	Canada	Salvation Army
The Rt Rev. J. E. L. Newbigin	U.K.	Church of South India
Professor C. G. W. Nicholls	Canada	Anglican Church of Canada
Dr R. E. Osborn	U.S.A.	Disciples of Christ (U.S.A.)
Professor R. S. Paul	U.S.A.	United Church of Christ (U.S.A.)
Dr P. E. Persson	Sweden	Church of Sweden
Bishop Pitirim of Volokolamsk	U.S.S.R.	Orthodox Church of Russia
The Rev. K. Rätsep	U.S.S.R.	Estonian Evangelical Lutheran Church
Dr H. G. Renkewitz	Germany	Evangelical Church in Germany (U)
Professor T. H. Runyon	U.S.A.	The Methodist Church (U.S.A.)
Professor V. Sarychev	U.S.S.R.	Orthodox Church of Russia
The Rev. T. S. Sihombing	Indonesia	Protestant Christian Batak Church
The Rev. R. G. Spaugh	U.S.A.	Moravian Church in America (Southern Province)
Dean C. S. Spivey, Jr	U.S.A.	African Methodist Episcopal Church
The Rev. E. Stephanou	U.S.A.	Greek Orthodox Archdiocese of N. and S. America, Ecumenical Patriarchate
Mr W. Stringfellow	U.S.A.	Protestant Episcopal Church (U.S.A.)
Dr M. Takenaka (*Secretary*)	Japan	United Church of Christ in Japan
Principal H. E. Thomas	Ghana	The Methodist Church, Ghana
Dr A. L. Tobing	Indonesia	Protestant Christian Batak Church
Professor V. Vinay (*Secretary*)	Italy	Waldensian Church (Italy)
Dr W. H. Weiblen	U.S.A.	The American Lutheran Church
Mr R. C. Young	Canada	United Church of Canada

SECTION IV: 'Worship and the Oneness of Christ's Church'

Professor H. Alivisatos	Greece	Church of Greece (Orthodox)
The Rt Rev. R. G. Arthur, Bishop of Grafton	Australia	Church of England in Australia
The Rev. E. L. Bader	Canada	Roman Catholic Church
Dr W. G. Baker	U.K.	Churches of Christ in Gt Britain and Ireland

The Rev. R. A. Balk	Canada	Protestant Episcopal Church (U.S.A.)
Professor B. Bobrinskoy	France	Russian Exarchate in Western Europe, Ecumenical Patriarchate
Commissioner W. Booth	Canada	Salvation Army
Dr W. R. Bouman	U.S.A.	Lutheran Church—Missouri Synod
The Rev. R. Breen	Canada	Roman Catholic Church
Dean F. R. Brown	U.S.A.	African Methodist Episcopal Zion Church
Bishop A. Buthi	Rumania	Transylvanian Reformed Church
The Rev. R. Cain	U.S.A.	The Methodist Church (U.S.A.)
Dr W. R. Cannon	U.S.A.	The Methodist Church (U.S.A.)
The Rev. S. Carile	Italy	Evangelical Methodist Church of Italy
The Rev. K. J. Carter	Australia	Methodist Church of Australasia
Principal J. R. Chandran (*Vice-Chairman*)	India	Church of South India
The Rev. E. Chavez Campos	Chile	Pentecostal Church of Chile
Dr L. H. Chow	Taiwan	Taiwan Baptist Convention
Mr T. J. Christenson	U.S.A.	The American Lutheran Church
The Most Rev. H. H. Clark, Primate of Canada	Canada	Anglican Church of Canada
The Ven. J. O. Cobham	U.K.	Church of England
The Rt Rev. W. R. Coleman, Bishop of Kootenay	Canada	Anglican Church of Canada
Dr M. A. Creasey	U.K.	London Yearly Meeting of the Society of Friends
Professor R. E. Cushman	U.S.A.	The Methodist Church (U.S.A.)
The Rev. G. Diekmann	U.S.A.	Roman Catholic Church
Dr F. W. Dillistone	U.K.	Church of England
Metropolitan Dorotheos of Castorias	Greece	Church of Greece (Orthodox)
The Rev. S. A. Farah	Lebanon	Evangelical Episcopal Church
The Rev. R. S. French	U.S.A.	Protestant Episcopal Church (U.S.A.)
Dr F. C. Fry	U.S.A.	Lutheran Church in America
The Rt Rev. M. V. Ga	Philippines	Philippine Independent Catholic Church
The Rev. F. S. Galvez	Philippines	Methodist Church in the Philippines
The Rev. J. G. Gatu	Kenya	Presbyterian Church of East Africa
Principal A. R. George	U.K.	Methodist Church in Gt Britain
Dr H. G. Hageman	U.S.A.	Reformed Church in America
Professor W. Hahn (*Vice-Chairman*)	Germany	Evangelical Church in Germany (L)
Dr R. B. Hannen	U.S.A.	American Baptist Convention
Professor E. R. Hardy	U.S.A.	Protestant Episcopal Church (U.S.A.)

Dr H. H. Harms (*Secretary*)	Germany	Evangelical Church in Germany (L)
Professor D. W. Hay	Canada	Presbyterian Church in Canada
Dr F. Herzog	U.S.A.	United Church of Christ (U.S.A.)
Professor H. A. Hodges	U.K.	Church of England
Dr P. E. Hughes	U.K.	Church of England
Dr D. R. Hunter	U.S.A.	Protestant Episcopal Church (U.S.A.)
The Rev. I. Ivanov	U.S.S.R.	Union of Evangelical Christian Baptists (U.S.S.R.)
Dr G. K. A. Jacob	Germany	Evangelical Church in Germany (U)
Miss H. Jaentti	Finland	Evangelical Lutheran Church of Finland
The Rt Rev. A. H. Johnston, Bishop of Dunedin	New Zealand	Church of the Province of New Zealand (Anglican)
Professor W. M. Kelly	Canada	United Church of Canada
The Rev. Y. Kishimoto	Japan	United Church of Christ in Japan
Dean P. Kleperis	U.S.S.R.	Evangelical Lutheran Church of Latvia
The Rev. E. Lamirande	Canada	Roman Catholic Church
Professor A. F. N. Lekkerkerker	Netherlands	Netherlands Reformed Church
Dr T. S. Liefeld	U.S.A.	The American Lutheran Church
The Rev. J. C. Lusk	U.K.	Church of Scotland
President J. I. McCord (*Chairman*)	U.S.A.	United Presbyterian Church (U.S.A.)
Professor J. Meyendorff (*Secretary*)	U.S.A.	Russian Orthodox Greek Catholic Church of America
The Rev. C. Matura	Canada	Roman Catholic Church
Metropolitan Nikodim of Sliven	Bulgaria	Bulgarian Orthodox Church
Dr E. A. Payne	U.K.	Baptist Union of Gt Britain and Ireland
The Rev. A. M. Pennybacker	U.S.A.	Disciples of Christ (U.S.A.)
The Rev. D. Peter	India	Federation of Evangelical Lutheran Churches in India
Dr A. Peters	Germany	Evangelical Church in Germany (L)
The Rev. K. Philipos	India	Orthodox Syrian Church of the East
The Rev. E. Pichal	Belgium	Evangelical Protestant Church of Belgium
Dr W. S. F. Pickering	Canada	Anglican Church of Canada
Principal H. Roberts	U.K.	Methodist Church in Gt Britain
The Very Rev. P. Rodopoulos	U.S.A.	Greek Orthodox Archdiocese of N. and S. America, Ecumenical Patriarchate
Professor A. Schmemann	U.S.A.	Russian Orthodox Greek Catholic Church of America
Professor J. A. Sittler (*Bible Study Leader*)	U.S.A.	Lutheran Church in America
The Rev. L. J. Steady	Canada	Roman Catholic Church

Bishop K. Støylen	Norway	Church of Norway
Bishop Theoctiste	Rumania	Rumanian Orthodox Church
Brother Max Thurian	France	Reformed Church of France
Dr T. N. Tice	U.S.A.	United Presbyterian Church (U.S.A.)
Professor N. Uspensky	U.S.S.R.	Orthodox Church of Russia
The Rev. T. P. Verghese	India	Orthodox Syrian Church of the East
Bishop Vladimir	U.S.S.R.	Orthodox Church of Russia
The Rev. K. Yamazato	Okinawa	United Church of Christ in Okinawa
The Rev. M. Zhidkov	U.S.S.R.	Union of Evangelical Christian Baptists (U.S.S.R.)
The Rt Rev. T. F. Zielinski	U.S.A.	Old Catholic Church of the Netherlands

Section V ' "All in Each Place": The Process of Growing Together'

The Rev. M. de Alwis	Ceylon	Church of India, Pakistan, Burma and Ceylon
Professor J. Beato	Brazil	Presbyterian Church of Brazil
The Rev. I. Beaubien	Canada	Roman Catholic Church
Miss E. L. Benignus	U.S.A.	Protestant Episcopal Church (U.S.A.)
The Rev. N. A. Berner	Canada	Lutheran Church in America
Dean W. B. Blakemore	U.S.A.	Disciples of Christ (U.S.A.)
Archpriest V. Borovoy	U.S.S.R.	Orthodox Church of Russia
Professor K. R. Bridston	U.S.A.	The American Lutheran Church
Professor J. A. Cardona	Puerto Rico	United Presbyterian Church (U.S.A.)
Principal L. G. Champion	U.K.	Baptist Union of Gt Britain and Ireland
Dr E. H. S. Chandler	U.S.A.	United Church of Christ (U.S.A.)
Professor A. C. Core	U.S.A.	Evangelical United Brethren Church
Mr C. Deller	U.S.A.	United Presbyterian Church (U.S.A.)
Mrs J. De New	Canada	Churches of Christ (Disciples), Canada
The Rev. L. Y. Dillener	India	United Church of N. India and Pakistan
Dr R. Dodds	U.S.A.	United Church of Christ (U.S.A.)
The Rev. E. Eenigenburg	U.S.A.	Reformed Church in America
Professor N. Ehrenström (*Vice-Chairman*)	U.S.A.	Lutheran Church in America
The Rev. P. A. El-Moharraky	Egypt	Coptic Orthodox Church
The Rev. A. G. Faraday	Canada	Presbyterian Church in Canada
Dr J. R. Fleming (*Secretary*)	Malaya	Church of Scotland
The Rt Rev. D. A. Garnsey, Bishop of Gippsland	Australia	Church of England in Australia

President H. Gezork	U.S.A.	American Baptist Convention
Professor J. M. Gustafson	U.S.A.	United Church of Christ (U.S.A.)
The Rev. J. T. Hardyman	Madagascar	Church of Christ in Madagascar
The Rt Rev. I. Hazim (*Secretary*)	Lebanon	Greek Orthodox Patriarchate of Antioch (Syria)
Dr P. S. Hitchcock	U.S.A.	United Presbyterian Church (U.S.A.)
The Rev. Gwenyth Hubble	U.K.	Baptist Union of Gt Britain and Ireland
The Rt Rev. H. R. Hunt, Suffragan Bishop of Toronto	Canada	Anglican Church of Canada
Metropolitan Iakovos of Philadelphia	Turkey	Ecumenical Patriarchate of Constantinople
Principal G. Johnston	Canada	United Church of Canada
The Rev. J. M. Kibira	Tanganyika	Evangelical Church of North-West Tanganyika (Lutheran)
The Rev. D. Kitagawa	U.S.A.	Protestant Episcopal Church (U.S.A.)
Dr K. Kitamori	Japan	United Church of Christ in Japan
Dr H. Krüger	Germany	Evangelical Church in Germany (L)
The Rev. B. Lambert	Canada	Roman Catholic Church
The Rev. J. S. Lawson	Dahomey	Evangelical Protestant Methodist Church of Dahomey-Togo
Bishop J. W. Lord	U.S.A.	The Methodist Church (U.S.A.)
The Rev. O. W. McCully	Canada	Churches of Christ (Disciples), Canada
The Rev. E. S. Mackay	Canada	Presbyterian Church in Canada
Professor Z. K. Matthews	South Africa	Church of the Province of South Africa (Anglican)
Mr T. Miyabe	Japan	United Church of Christ in Japan
Dr L. S. Mudge	U.S.A.	United Presbyterian Church (U.S.A.)
Dean W. G. Muelder (*Chairman*)	U.S.A.	The Methodist Church (U.S.A.)
The Rev. E. O'Brien	Canada	Roman Catholic Church
The Rev. D. M. Paton	U.K.	Church of England
The Rev. F. A. W. Peacock	U.K.	Moravian Church in Gt Britain and Ireland
The Rt Rev. E. S. Reed, Bishop of Ottawa	Canada	Anglican Church of Canada
The Rev. P. C. Rodger	U.K.	Episcopal Church in Scotland
Mr E. Sa'aga	Samoa	Congregational Christian Church in Samoa
Canon H. A. E. Sawyerr	Sierra Leone	Church of the Province of West Africa (Anglican)
Dr F. Schlingensiepen	Germany	Evangelical Church in Germany (U)
Professor F. A. Shippey	U.S.A.	The Methodist Church (U.S.A.)

Bishop F. Sigg (*Bible Study Leader*)	Switzerland	The Methodist Church (U.S.A.)
The Rev. F. S. de Silva	Ceylon	Methodist Church in Ceylon
Professor A. M. Spaulding	U.S.A.	African Methodist Episcopal Zion Church
The Rev. I. O. A. Ude	Nigeria	Presbyterian Church of Nigeria
The Rev. J. J. Ulster	South Africa	Moravian Church in the Western Cape Province (S. Africa)
Bishop E. Varga (*Vice-Chairman*)	Czechoslovakia	Reformed Christian Church in Slovakia
The Rev. G. S. de Veiga	Brazil	Methodist Church of Brazil
The Rev. O. A. Waltner	U.S.A.	The General Conference Mennonite Church
The Rev. J. N. Ward	U.K.	Methodist Church in Gt Britain
The Rev. J. G. Weller	U.K.	Congregational Union of England and Wales
The Rt Rev. M. Wiggins, Bishop of Victoria Nyanza	Tanganyika	Church of the Province of East Africa (Anglican)
The Rev. K. S. Wills	Canada	Churches of Christ (Disciples), Canada
Professor G. F. Wingren	Sweden	Church of Sweden

NOT ALLOCATED TO SECTIONS

Dr R. P. Barnes	U.S.A.	United Presbyterian Church (U.S.A.)
The Rev. P. Davison	Canada	Anglican Church of Canada
The Rt Rev. M. Howard	Canada	Greek Orthodox Patriarchate of Antioch
The Rev. N. Jebejian	U.S.A.	Armenian Apostolic Church
The Rev. J. Long	U.S.A.	Roman Catholic Church
Professor T. R. Millman	Canada	Anglican Church of Canada
Mr B. Nelyubin	U.S.S.R.	Orthodox Church of Russia
The Rev. G. Ramlawy	Canada	Greek Orthodox Patriarchate of Antioch
Dr J. H. Satterwhite	U.S.A.	African Methodist Episcopal Zion Church
The Rev. C. R. Scovel	U.S.A.	Unitarian Universalist Association
The Rt Rev. O. S. Tomkins, Bishop of Bristol	U.K.	Church of England
Dr W. A. Visser 't Hooft	Netherlands	Netherlands Reformed Church

6

PARTICIPANTS IN THE CONFERENCE

* Indicates Church not a member of World Council of Churches.

AFRICA

CAMEROUN
*Presbyterian Church of Cameroun
  Adviser: Dr D. Gelzer

CENTRAL AFRICA
Church of the Province of Central Africa
  Delegate: The Rt Rev. C. Alderson, Bishop of Mashonaland
United Church of Central Africa in Rhodesia
  Delegate: The Rev. G. S. Smith
  Youth Del.:   The Rev. D. S. Sumbwanayambe

EAST AFRICA
Church of the Province of East Africa
  Delegate: The Rt Rev. M. Wiggins, Bishop of Victoria Nyanza
Evangelical Church of North-West Tanganyika (Lutheran)
  Delegate: The Rev. J. Kibira
Presbyterian Church of East Africa
  Delegate   The Rev. J. Gatu

EGYPT
Coptic Orthodox Church
  Delegate: The Rev. P. A. El-Moharraky

GHANA
Evangelical Presbyterian Church of Ghana
  Delegate: Mr F. Kokuma
The Methodist Church, Ghana
  Delegate: Principal H. E. Thomas
Presbyterian Church of Ghana
  Delegate: Mr N. O. Anim (*not present*)

MADAGASCAR
Church of Christ in Madagascar
  Delegate: The Rev. J. T. Hardyman

NIGERIA
Presbyterian Church of Nigeria
  Delegate: The Rev. I. O. A. Ude

SOUTH AFRICA
Church of the Province of South Africa
  Delegate: The Rt Rev. T. G. V. Inman, Bishop of Natal
Evangelical Lutheran Church in Southern Africa—South-East Region
  Delegate: The Rev. J. E. Farup

SOUTH AFRICA—*continued*
Moravian Church in Western Cape Province
   Delegate: The Rev. J. J. Ulster

TOGO
Evangelical Church of Togo
   Delegate: The Rev. S. Nomenyo (*not present*)

WEST AFRICA
Church of the Province of West Africa
   Delegate: Canon H. A. E. Sawyerr

AMERICA—NORTH

CANADA
Anglican Church of Canada
   Delegates: Professor E. R. Fairweather
                  Archdeacon R. K. Naylor
                  Professor H. H. Walsh
   Advisers: Professor C. G. W. Nicholls
                  Professor W. S. F. Pickering
   Youth Del.:   Mr D. Grayston
*Baptist Federation of Canada
   Adviser: Professor R. F. Aldwinckle
Churches of Christ (Disciples)
   Delegates: The Rev. O. W. McCully
                  The Rev. K. S. Wills
   Youth Del.:   Mrs J. De New
*Pentecostal Assemblies of Canada
   Observer: The Rev. R. M. Argue (*not present*)
Presbyterian Church in Canada
   Delegates: The Rev. S. B. Coles
                  Professor D. W. Hay
   Adviser: The Rev. G. C. Dalzell
   Youth Del.:   Mr F. Caloren
United Church of Canada
   Delegates: Dr R. C. Chalmers
                  Professor W. O. Fennell
                  Professor W. M. Kelly
   Advisers: Professor G. R. Cragg
                  Dr W. J. Gallagher
                  Principal G. Johnston
   Youth Del.:   Mr G. Cram

UNITED STATES
*Advent Christian General Conference of America
   Observer: Dr M. C. Crouse
African Methodist Episcopal Church
   Delegate: Dean C. S. Spivey, Jr
African Methodist Episcopal Zion Church
   Delegates: Dean F. R. Brown
                  Professor A. M. Spaulding
American Baptist Convention
   Delegates: President H. Gezork
                  Dr R. B. Hannen
                  Dr B. L. Ramm
                  Professor J. E. Skoglund
                  Dr H. H. Straton
   Adviser: Dr C. F. H. Henry

UNITED STATES—continued

American Lutheran Church
Delegates: Professor K. R. Bridston
Dr K. S. Knutson
Dr T. S. Liefeld
Dr W. H. Weiblen
Youth Del.: Mr T. J. Christenson

Armenian Apostolic Church
Delegate: Archbishop Tiran (Nersoyan)

*Christian Reformed Church
Observer: Dr F. H. Klooster

*Church of God (Anderson, Indiana)
Delegate: Dr E. Newberry
Observers: The Rev. L. Meyer
Dr J. W. V. Smith

Church of the Brethren
Delegate: Professor W. F. Groff

Disciples of Christ
Delegates: The Rev. G. G. Beazley, Jr
Dr W. B. Blakemore
Dr R. E. Osborn
The Rev. A. M. Pennybacker

Evangelical United Brethren Church
Delegates: Dr W. K. Clymer
Professor A. C. Core

*General Conference Mennonite Church
Observer: The Rev. O. A. Waltner
Adviser: Dr J. H. Yoder

*General Conference of Seventh Day Adventists
Observer: The Rev. H. W. Lowe

Greek Orthodox Archdiocese of North and South America (Ecumenical Patriarchate)
Delegates: Metropolitan Athenagoras of Elaia
Professor G. Florovsky
Archimandrite P. E. Rodopoulos
Professor J. S. Romanides
The Rev. E. Stephanou

Hungarian Reformed Church in America
Delegate: The Rev. A. Komjathy

Lutheran Church in America
Delegates: Professor S. E. Ahlstrom
Dr C. J. I. Bergendoff
Professor N. Ehrenström
Dr J. Knudsen
Dr W. H. Lazareth
Dr U. S. Leupold
Professor J. Sittler
Dr W. J. Villaume
Adviser: Professor G. Lindbeck

*The Lutheran Church—Missouri Synod
Observers: Dr P. M. Bretscher
Dr R. Jungkuntz
The Rev. D. Pourchot

The Methodist Church
Delegates: Dr R. Cain
Dr W. R. Cannon
Dr R. E. Cushman
Bishop F. G. Ensley (*not present*)
Dr J. Gonzales (Puerto Rico)
Bishop J. W. Lord

UNITED STATES—continued
The Methodist Church—continued

Dr G. O. McCulloh
Dean W. G. Muelder
Professor J. R. Nelson
Professor A. C. Outler
Dr J. Radha Krishan (India)
Professor F. A. Shippey
Bishop F. Sigg (North and Central Europe)
Professor C. Welch

Adviser: The Rev. D. S. Green

Moravian Church in America (Northern Province)
Delegate: Professor V. W. Couillard
Moravian Church in America (Southern Province)
Delegate: The Rev. R. G. Spaugh
National Baptist Convention of America
Delegate: The Rev. N. S. Jones (*not present*)
North American Baptist General Conference
Observer: Professor G. A. Dunger
Polish National Catholic Church of America
Delegate: The Rev. E. Magyar (*not present*)
Presbyterian Church in the United States
Delegates: Dr R. H. Bullock
Dr J. N. Thomas
Protestant Episcopal Church in the U.S.A.
Delegates: The Rt Rev. S. F. Bayne (*not present*)
Dean J. B. Coburn
Professor E. R. Hardy
The Rev. Dr S. F. Nishi
The Rt Rev. P. L. Simoes (Brazil)
Mr W. Stringfellow
Advisers: Bishop A. Dun
The Rev. Dr F. W. Tomkins
Reformed Church in America
Delegates: The Rev. E. Eenigenburg
The Rev. H. G. Hageman
Religious Society of Friends: Friends General Conference
Delegate: Mr D. Freiday
Russian Orthodox Greek Catholic Church of America
Delegates: The Rev. W. Berzonsky
Professor A. Schmemann
Adviser: Professor J. Meyendorff
Seventh Day Baptist General Conference
Delegate: The Rev. L. F. Hurley
Southern Baptist Convention
Adviser: Professor D. Moody
Syrian Antiochian Orthodox Church
Delegate: The Rev. W. S. Schneirla (*not present*)
United Church of Christ
Delegates: Professor E. F. J. Arndt
Professor J. M. Gustafson
Dr F. Herzog
Dr R. D. Hyslop
Adviser: Dr R. S. Paul
United Presbyterian Church in the U.S.A.
Delegates: Dr F. V. Filson
Dr P. S. Hitchcock
Dr R. C. Johnson
Dr J. Larson
President J. I. McCord

UNITED STATES—continued
United Presbyterian Church in the U.S.A.—continued

Dr T. M. Taylor
Advisers: Dr E. C. Blake

Dr T. N. Tice
Youth Del.: Mr C. Deller

AMERICA—SOUTH AND CARIBBEAN

ARGENTINA
United Evangelical Lutheran Church in Argentina
Delegate: Dr B. Lesko

BRAZIL
Armenian Evangelical Church
Adviser: The Rev. A. Sapsezian
Methodist Church of Brazil
Delegate: The Rev. G. S. de Veiga
Presbyterian Church of Brazil
Adviser: Dr J. Beato

CHILE
Pentecostal Church of Chile
Delegate: The Rev. E. Chavez Campos

MEXICO
Congregational Church of Mexico
Youth Del.: Professor E. Guerra

TRINIDAD
Presbyterian Church in Trinidad
Delegate: The Rev. J. F. Seunarine

URUGUAY
Lutheran Church in Uruguay
Adviser: Dr A. E. Fernandez Arlt
Waldensian Church of Rio de la Plata
Adviser: The Rev. W. Artus

WEST INDIES
Church of the Province of the West Indies
Delegate: The Rt Rev. B. N. Y. Vaughan, Bishop of Mandeville
Presbyterian Church of Jamaica
Delegate: The Rt Rev. D. R. Miller

ASIA (*including Near East*)

BURMA
Burma Baptist Convention
Adviser: The Rev. P. D. Clasper

CEYLON
Methodist Church in Ceylon
Delegate: The Rev. F. S. de Silva

INDIA
Church of India, Pakistan, Burma and Ceylon
   Delegates: Canon J. Maung Pe (Burma)
                   Archdeacon H. de Soysa (Ceylon) (*not present*)
   Youth Del.:   The Rev. M. de Alwis (Ceylon)
Church of South India
   Delegates: Principal J. R. Chandran
                   The Rev. K. M. John
Federation of Evangelical Lutheran Churches in India
   Delegates: The Rev. N. Minz (*not present*)
                   The Rev. D. Peter
Mar Thoma Syrian Church of Malabar
   Delegate: The Rt Rev. T. Mar Athanasius
Orthodox Syrian Church of the East
   Delegates: The Rev. K. Philipos
                   Professor V. C. Samuel
United Church of Northern India and Pakistan
   Delegate: The Rev. L. Y. Dillener

INDONESIA
Christian Churches in Mid-Java
   Delegate: The Rev. B. Probowinoto
Protestant Christian Batak Church
   Delegates: The Rev. T. S. Sihombing
                   Dr A. L. Tobing

JAPAN
**Japan Evangelical Lutheran Church*
   Delegate: Dr C. Kishi
*Mukyokai (*Non-Church Movement*)
   Adviser: Dr G. Mayeda
Nippon Sei Ko Kai (*Anglican*)
   Delegate: The Rev. J. T. Yashiro
United Church of Christ in Japan
   Delegate: Dr K. Kitamori
   Advisers: Professor M. Doi
                   Dr M. Takenaka
   Youth Del.:   Mr T. Miyabe

KOREA
Presbyterian Church in the Republic of Korea
   Adviser: Dr Kim Chai Choon

LEBANON
Armenian Apostolic Church (*Catholicosate of Cilicia*)
   Adviser: The Very Rev. K. V. Sarkissian
Greek Orthodox Patriarchate of Antioch (*Syria*)
   Adviser: The Rt Rev. I. Hazim, Bishop of Palmyra
Union of Armenian Evangelical Churches in the Near East
   Delegate: Dr J. J. Markarian

PAKISTAN
United Presbyterian Church of Pakistan
   Delegate: Dr K. L. Nasir

PHILIPPINES
Philippine Independent Catholic Church
   Delegate: The Rt Rev. M. V. Ga, Bishop of Negros and Siquijor
United Church of Christ in the Philippines
   Delegate: Bishop O. G. Fonceca

TAIWAN
Presbyterian Church in Formosa
　　Adviser:　　　　　Dr C. H. Hwang
*Taiwan Baptist Convention
　　Adviser:　　　　　Dr L. H. Chow

TURKEY
Ecumenical Patriarchate of Constantinople
　　Delegates:　　　　Metropolitan Chrysostomos of Myra
　　　　　　　　　　Metropolitan Iakovos of Philadelphia
　　　　　　　　　　Metropolitan Meliton of Heliopolis

AUSTRALASIA

AUSTRALIA
Church of England in Australia
　　Delegates:　　　　The Rt Rev. R. G. Arthur, Bishop of Grafton
　　　　　　　　　　The Rt Rev. D. A. Garnsey, Bishop of Gippsland
Federal Conference of Churches of Christ in Australia
　　Delegate:　　　　Dr K. R. Bowes
Methodist Church in Australasia
　　Delegate:　　　　The Rev. K. J. Carter
　　Youth Del.:　　　Mr D'A. Wood
Presbyterian Church of Australia
　　Delegate:　　　　Professor J. D. McCaughey

NEW CALEDONIA
Evangelical Church in New Caledonia and the Loyalty Isles
　　Delegate:　　　　Pastor M.-A. Ledoux

NEW ZEALAND
Associated Churches of Christ in New Zealand
　　Delegate:　　　　Dr A. B. McDiarmid
Methodist Church of New Zealand
　　Delegate:　　　　The Rev. L. P. Schroeder
Presbyterian Church of New Zealand
　　Delegate:　　　　The Rev. J. M. Bates

SAMOA
Congregational Christian Church in Samoa
　　Delegate:　　　　Mr E. Sa'aga

EUROPE

AUSTRIA
Evangelische Kirche A.u.H.B. in Oesterreich
　　Delegate:　　　　Professor W. Dantine

BELGIUM
Evangelical Protestant Church of Belgium
　　Delegate:　　　　Pastor E. Pichal

BULGARIA
Bulgarian Orthodox Church
　　Delegate:　　　　Metropolitan Nikodim of Sliven

CYPRUS
Church of Cyprus
　　Delegate:　　　　Professor H. Alivisatos (Church of Greece)

CZECHOSLOVAKIA
Evangelical Church of Czech Brethren
Delegate: Dr J. Smolik
Evangelical Church in Slovakia, Augsburg Confession
Delegate: Dr J. Michalko
Reformed Christian Church in Slovakia
Delegate: Bishop E. Varga

DENMARK
Church of Denmark
Delegates: Professor J. M. Aagaard
Professor N. H. Søe

FINLAND
Evangelical Lutheran Church of Finland
Delegate: Dr S. A. Teinonen
Youth Del.: Miss H. Jaentti
Orthodox Church in Finland (Ecumenical Patriarchate)
Adviser: The Rev. N. Karjomaa

FRANCE
Evangelical Church of Augsburg Confession in Alsace and Lorraine
Delegate: Professor A. Benoît
Reformed Church of Alsace and Lorraine
Delegate: Professor R. Mehl
Reformed Church of France
Delegate: Professor J. Bosc
Adviser: Frère M. Thurian (Taizé Community)
Russian Exarchate in Western Europe (Ecumenical Patriarchate)
Adviser: Professor B. Bobrinskoy

GERMANY
Altkatholische Kirche in Deutschland (Old Catholic Church)
Delegate: Professor W. F. A. Küppers
Evangelische Brüder-Unität (Moravian Church)
Delegate: The Rev. H.-C. Hahn
Evangelische Kirche in Deutschland
Delegates: (Lutheran) Dr H. Beintker (D.D.R.)
Dr H. H. Harms
Professor W. Joest
Professor F. W. Kantzenbach
Dr W. Krusche (D.D.R.) (*not present*)
Dr A. Peters
Dr H. F. Pflugk (D.D.R.) (*not present*)
(United) Professor E. Dinkler
The Rev. J. Hamel (D.D.R.) (*not present*)
Dr G. Jacob (D.D.R.)
Dr H. Reiss
Dr H. Renkewitz
Dr F. Schlingensiepen
(Reformed) Professor J. Moltmann
Professor W. Niesel
Advisers: Professor W. Hahn
Professor E. Käsemann
Dr R. Slenczka
Youth Del.: The Rev. J. Kleeman

GREECE
Church of Greece
Delegates: Professor H. Alivisatos (also representing the Church of
Cyprus)

GREECE—*continued*

Metropolitan Cyprian of Monemvasias and Spartis
Metropolitan Damascenos of Demetriados
Metropolitan Dorotheos of Castorias
Metropolitan Iakovos of Elassonos
Professor G. Konidaris

ITALY
Evangelical Methodist Church of Italy
  Delegate: Pastor S. Carile
*Roman Catholic Church
  Observers: The Rev. G. Baum (Canada)
                 The Rev. G. Diekmann (U.S.A.)
                 Professor J. C. Groot (Netherlands)
                 The Rev. B. Lambert (Canada)
                 The Rev. G. Tavard (U.S.A.)
Waldensian Church
  Delegate: Professor V. Vinay

NETHERLANDS
General Mennonite Society
  Delegate: Professor J. A. Oosterbaan
Netherlands Reformed Church
  Delegates: Professor A. J. Bronkhorst
                 Professor A. F. N. Lekkerkerker
  Adviser: Dr E. Flesseman-van Leer
  Youth Del.:   Mr P. P. van Lelyveld
Old Catholic Church
  Delegate: The Rt Rev. T. F. Zielinski (Polish National Catholic
                                             Church of America)
Remonstrant Brotherhood
  Delegate: The Rev. A. M. van Peski

NORWAY
Church of Norway
  Delegates: Dr H. Flottorp
                 Professor E. Molland
                 Bishop K. Stöylen

RUMANIA
Evangelical Lutheran Church of Augsburg Confession
  Delegate: Dr H. Binder (*not present*)
Rumanian Orthodox Church
  Delegates: Professor N. Chitescu
                 Metropolitan Justin of Moldavia
                 The Rev. N. Nicolaescu
                 Mgr Theoctiste
Transylvanian Reformed Church
  Delegate: Bishop A. Buthi

SWEDEN
Church of Sweden
  Delegates: Dr R. Holte
                 Bishop A. Nygren
                 Dr P. E. Persson
                 Professor G. F. Wingren

SWITZERLAND
Old Catholic Church
  Delegate: Professor A. E. Rüthy (*not present*)

H

SWITZERLAND—continued

Swiss Protestant Church Federation
Delegates: Professor H. D'Espine
                  Professor E. Schweizer
Advisers: Professor J.-J. von Allmen
                  Professor J.-L. Leuba

UNITED KINGDOM
Baptist Union of Great Britain and Ireland
Delegates: Principal L. G. Champion
                  Dr E. A. Payne
Adviser: Dr G. R. Beasley-Murray
Church of England
Delegates: The Rev. A. M. Allchin
                  The Ven. J. O. Cobham
                  Dr F. W. Dillistone
                  Professor S. L. Greenslade
                  Professor H. A. Hodges
                  Miss R. C. Howard
                  Dr P. E. Hughes
                  The Rt Rev. O. S. Tomkins, Bishop of Bristol
                  Canon H. M. Waddams
Advisers: The Rt Rev. A. M. Hollis
                  Professor G. W. H. Lampe
Youth Del.:   Mr M. J. Gudgeon
Church of Ireland
Delegate: Professor H. F. Woodhouse
Church of Scotland
Delegates: Dr I. M. Fraser
                  The Rev. J. C. Lusk
                  Professor J. K. S. Reid
Adviser: Dr J. R. Fleming
Church in Wales
Delegate: The Rt Rev. G. O. Williams, Bishop of Bangor
Churches of Christ in Great Britain and Ireland
Delegate: Dr W. G. Baker (also representing the Congregational Union
                                                      of Scotland)
Congregational Union of England and Wales
Delegate: The Rev. J. P. Lee-Woolf
Congregational Union of Scotland
Delegate: Dr W. G. Baker (Churches of Christ in Gt Britain and
                                                      Ireland)
Episcopal Church in Scotland
Delegate: The Very Rev. A. I. M. Haggart (*not present*)
***London Yearly Meeting of the Society of Friends**
Delegate: Dr M. A. Creasey
Methodist Church in Great Britain
Delegates: The Rev. R. E. Davies
                  Principal A. R. George
                  Principal H. Roberts
                  The Rev. J. N. Ward
Youth Del.:   The Rev. Dr J. Newton
Methodist Church in Ireland
Delegate: The Rev. R. A. Nelson
Moravian Church in Great Britain and Ireland
Delegate: The Rev. F. A. W. Peacock
Presbyterian Church of England
Delegate: Mr J. M. Ross
Presbyterian Church in Ireland
Delegate: The Very Rev. Dr A. A. Fulton

UNITED KINGDOM—*continued*
The Salvation Army
Delegates: Commissioner W. Booth (Canada)
                Commissioner S. Hepburn (U.S.A.)
                Lt-Col P. S. Kaiser (U.S.A.)
                Lt-Col G. Moulton (Canada)

U.S.S.R.
Esthonian Lutheran Church
Delegate: The Rev. J. Rätsep
Evangelical Lutheran Church of Latvia
Delegate: Dean P. Kleperis
Orthodox Church of Russia (Patriarchate of Moscow)
Delegates: Archbishop Basile
                Archpriest V. Borovoy
                Mr A. Buevsky
                Archbishop John
                Archimandrite Pitirim
                Professor V. Sarychev
                Archpriest I. W. Susemihl
                Professor N. D. Uspensky
                Bishop Vladimir
                Archpriest L. Voronov
Union of Evangelical Christian Baptists of the USSR
Delegates: The Rev. I. Ivanov
                The Rev. J. Zhidkov (*not present*)
                The Rev. M. Zhidkov

YUGOSLAVIA
**Serbian Orthodox Church*
Observer: The Very Rev. D. F. Najdanovich (Canada)

Esthonian Evangelical Lutheran Church in Exile
Delegate: The Rev. B. Ederma

OTHER PARTICIPANTS

Ex Officio

The Rev. Prof. R. E. Brown	U.S.A.	*Roman Catholic Church
The Most Rev. H. H. Clark, Primate of Canada	Canada	Anglican Church of Canada
Dr F. C. Fry	U.S.A.	Lutheran Church in America
Dr D. Horton	U.S.A.	United Church of Christ (U.S.A.)

Faith and Order Secretaries

The Rev. S. K. Bunker	National Christian Council of Ceylon	Church of South India

The Rev. S. A. Farah	Near East Christian
	  Council
		Evangelical Episcopal
		  Church

Dr H. Krüger	Oekumenische Centrale	Evangelical Church in Germany
The Rev. J. S. Lawson	All Africa Conference of Churches	*Evangelical Protestant Methodist Church of Dahomey-Togo
The Rev. W. A. Norgren	National Council of the Churches of Christ U.S.A.	Protestant Episcopal Church (U.S.A.)
The Rev. J. G. Weller	British Council of Churches	Congregational Union of England and Wales

Guests

The Rev. E. L. Bader	Canada	*Roman Catholic Church
The Rev. R. A. Balk	Canada	Protestant Episcopal Church (U.S.A.)
The Rev. I. Beaubien	Canada	*Roman Catholic Church
Miss E. L. Benignus	U.S.A.	Protestant Episcopal Church (U.S.A.)
The Rev. N. A. Berner	Canada	Lutheran Church in America
Dr W. R. Bouman	U.S.A.	Lutheran Church—Missouri Synod
The Rev. R. Breen	Canada	*Roman Catholic Church
Mrs Porter Brown	U.S.A.	The Methodist Church (U.S.A.)
The Rev. A. Brunet	Canada	*Roman Catholic Church
Professor J. A. Cardona	Puerto Rico	United Presbyterian Church (U.S.A.)
Dr E. H. S. Chandler	U.S.A.	United Church of Christ (U.S.A.)
The Rt Rev. W. R. Coleman, Bishop of Kootenay	Canada	Anglican Church of Canada
Dr P. A. Crow, Jr	U.S.A.	Disciples of Christ (U.S.A.)
Dr M. E. Culver	U.S.A.	The Methodist Church (U.S.A.)
The Rev. P. Davison	Canada	Anglican Church of Canada
Professor P. De Jong	Canada	United Church of Canada
The Rev. H. M. De Wolfe	Canada	*Baptist Federation of Canada
Dr R. Dodds	U.S.A.	United Church of Christ (U.S.A.)
The Rev. J. Drew	U.S.A.	*Roman Catholic Church
The Rev. A. G. Faraday	Canada	Presbyterian Church in Canada
The Rev. E. E. Hallman	Canada	Evangelical United Brethren Church
Professor J. W. Heikkinen	U.S.A.	Lutheran Church in America
Rabbi P. Hiat	U.S.A.	*Synagogue Council of America
Miss K. B. Hockin	Canada	United Church of Canada
The Rev. J. R. Hord	Canada	United Church of Canada
Dr W. M. Horton	U.S.A.	United Church of Christ (U.S.A.)
The Rt Rev. M. Howard	Canada	Greek Orthodox Patriarchate of Antioch
The Rt Rev. H. R. Hunt, Suffragan Bishop of Toronto	Canada	Anglican Church of Canada
Dr L. Hunt	Canada	Anglican Church of Canada
Dr D. R. Hunter	U.S.A.	Protestant Episcopal Church (U.S.A.)
The Rev. N. Jebejian	U.S.A.	Armenian Apostolic Church
Dr J. A. Johnson, Jr	U.S.A.	Christian Methodist Episcopal Church

The Rt Rev. A. H. Johnston, Bishop of Dunedin	New Zealand	Church of the Province of New Zealand
Professor C. F. Johnston	Canada	United Church of Canada
The Rev. Y. Kishimoto	Japan	United Church of Christ in Japan
The Rev. P. L. Kjeseth	U.S.A.	The American Lutheran Church
The Rev. E. Lamirande	Canada	*Roman Catholic Church
The Rev. W. A. Landman	South Africa	*Dutch Reformed Church in S. Africa
The Rev. G. Langevin	Canada	*Roman Catholic Church
Dr T. A. Langford	U.S.A.	The Methodist Church (U.S.A.)
The Rev. J.-M. Langlais	Canada	*Roman Catholic Church
The Rev. M. Lefebvre	Canada	*Roman Catholic Church
The Rev. J. Long	U.S.A.	*Roman Catholic Church
The Rev. S. Macdonnell	Canada	Presbyterian Church in Canada
The Rev. E. S. Mackay	Canada	Presbyterian Church in Canada
The Rev. J. Martucci	Canada	*Roman Catholic Church
Professor D. M. Mathers	Canada	United Church of Canada
The Rev. C. Matura	Canada	*Roman Catholic Church
Professor T. R. Millman	Canada	Anglican Church of Canada
Dr L. S. Mudge	U.S.A.	United Presbyterian Church (U.S.A.)
Mr B. Nelyubin	U.S.S.R.	Orthodox Church of Russia
The Rev. E. O'Brien	Canada	*Roman Catholic Church
Dr H. J. Ockenga	U.S.A.	*Congregational
The Rev. D. J. O'Hanlon	U.S.A.	*Roman Catholic Church
The Rev. B. J. O'Keefe	Canada	*Roman Catholic Church
Dr W. Quanbeck	U.S.A.	The American Lutheran Church
The Rev. G. Ramlawy	Canada	Greek Orthodox Patriarchate of Antioch
The Rev. E. C. Reckard	U.S.A.	United Presbyterian Church (U.S.A.)
The Rt Rev. E. S. Reed, Bishop of Ottawa	Canada	Anglican Church of Canada
Professor T. H. Runyon	U.S.A.	The Methodist Church (U.S.A.)
Dr J. H. Satterwhite	U.S.A.	African Methodist Episcopal Zion Church
The Rev. C. R. Scovel	U.S.A.	*Unitarian Universalist Association
The Rev. L. J. Steady	Canada	*Roman Catholic Church
Dr G. A. Thiele	U.S.A.	*Lutheran Church—Missouri Synod
Dr R. Tobias	U.S.A.	——
Professor C. K. Von Euw	U.S.A.	*Roman Catholic Church
Professor J. W. Winterhager	Germany	Evangelical Church in Germany
The Rev. K. Yamazato	Okinawa	United Church of Christ in Okinawa

FRATERNAL REPRESENTATIVES

International Association for Liberal Christianity and Religious Freedom	The Rev. A. M. van Peski
International Congregational Council	Dr Douglas Horton
World Alliance of Reformed Churches (World Presbyterian Alliance)	President J. I. McCord
World Alliance of Y.M.C.A.'s	Dr A. E. Fernandez Arlt
World Convention of Churches of Christ	Dr W. G. Baker
World Council of Christian Education and Sunday School Association	Dr David R. Hunter

World Student Christian Federation   Mr F. Caloren
     Mr D. Martin Conway
     The Rev. M. de Alwis
World Y.W.C.A.   Miss Katherine Hockin

Montreal Committee on Arrangements

Executive Committee:
Principal G. Johnston (*Chairman*)
The Rev. G. C. Dalzell (*Secretary*)
Dean S. B. Frost
Canon R. R. Latimer
Dr W. J. Gallagher
Dr E. E. Long

Sub-Committee Chairmen:

Arrangements with McGill University:	Dean S. B. Frost
Reception and Transportation:	Mrs J. De New
Social Events:	Miss D. Blaise
Local Church Arrangements:	Canon R. R. Latimer
Press and Public Relations:	Dr D. J. Wilson
Radio and Television:	Professor C. R. Bell
Finance:	Mr D. B. Peters
Consultations:	Principal E. G. Jay
Ecumenical Rally Special Committee:	Father I. Beaubien, S.J.

Staff

WCC Executive Staff

Dr R. P. Barnes	Professor P. S. Minear
Dr R. S. Bilheimer	Bishop J. E. L. Newbigin
The Rev. W. H. Clark	Dr N. A. Nissiotis
The Rev. R. S. French	The Rev. P. C. Rodger
The Rev. M. B. Handspicker	Mr A. Schneider
The Rev. V. E. W. Hayward	The Rev. Fr P. Verghese
The Rev. Gwenyth Hubble	Dr L. Vischer
Miss F. Maeda	Dr W. A. Visser 't Hooft
Professor Z. K. Matthews	Dr H. H. Wolf
The Rev. R. E. Maxwell	Mr R. C. Young

Co-opted Staff: The Rev. D. Kitagawa
The Rev. D. M. Paton

Press and Information
Mr P. Maury
Mr J. Taylor
Miss B. Thompson

Mrs H. Boyens	Mr L. Heins
Miss W. Buchanan	Mr L. McMaster
Mr P. Carlson	Mr A. J. Moore
Miss J. Dardel	Mrs C. O'Neal
The Rev. G. Heidtmann	Mr N. Vale

Translation and Interpretation
The Rev. A. Boyens

The Rev. J. R. Arnold	Mr D. M. Conway
Miss K. Benckert	The Rev. C. B. R. de Mestral
The Rev. H. Birchmeier	The Rev. E. de Peyer
The Rev. R. Brecheisen	The Rev. G. A. Deschamps

Miss E. M. Evans
Mrs T. Evdokimov
Mr E. Frerichs
Miss I. Friedeberg
The Rev. E. J. Furcha
Dr G. Gassmann
Mrs U. Gassmann
The Rev. F. C. Gérard
The Rev. M. A. Goertz
The Rev. A. Harvey
The Rev. H. H. Hirschberg
Mrs E. Lauber
Mr P. H. Luciri

The Rev. H. K. Maurer
The Rev. A. Mobbs
The Rev. M. Ouellet
The Rev. A. Plag
Mr B. Sartorius
Mr K. L. Simon
Miss I. Soltau
Mr H. D. Stollberg
Mr R. D. Thoma
The Rev. D. Tustin
Dr G. Wagner
The Rev. W. A. Wright

Conference Staff

Headquarters Office: Miss S. Frazer
Miss A. Guittart
Miss E. Swayne

Typing and Document Office: Mrs M. Burton
Mrs H. Dunant
Miss A. Eikenberg
Miss E. Imbescheidt
Miss E. Jacot
Miss W. Les

Miss M. Monier
Miss I. Panning
Miss H. Schmal
Miss B. Sterzel
Miss S. Zahar

Stewards
Dr H. P. Nebelsick

Mr D. W. Chappell
Mr J. S. Couling
The Rev. T. E. Dipko
Mrs S. Dipko
Mr D. W. Davis
Miss K. M. Kitagawa
Mr J. D. Liles
Mr R. K. Loesch
Mrs B. Loesch
Miss J. Lynch

The Rev. D. S. MacDonald
Mr J. G. Maheras
The Rev. D. A. Metzler
The Rev. G. Millard
The Rev. V. M. Newton
The Rev. J. D. Riddle
Miss D. R. Runnalls
Miss J. I. Smith
Mr G. A. Weckman

7

ANALYSIS OF THE MEMBERSHIP

	AFRICA	N. AMERICA	S. AMERICA AND CARIBBEAN	ASIA AND NR EAST	AUSTRALASIA	EUROPE	
Delegates	14(2)	84(5)	8	23(2)	10	93(7)	232(16)
Advisers	1	18(1)	4	10	—	13	46(1)
Observers	—	15(1)	—	—	—	1	16(1)
Youth Del.	1	6	1	2	1	5	16
F. & O. Secs.	1	1	—	2	—	2	6
Ex officio	—	4	—	—	—	—	4
Guests	1	61	1	2	1	2	68
Staff	1	50	—	2	—	48	101
	19(2)	239(7)	14	41(2)	12	164(7)	489(18)

Figures in brackets indicate delegates or observers who were appointed but were unable to attend the Conference.

INDEX OF SUBJECTS

Publications in Connection with the Fourth World Conference on Faith and Order

Montreal—1963

Faith and Order Findings

The report to the Fourth World Conference on Faith and Order, ed. Paul Minear. SCM Press, London, 1963. 21s. (available from Publication Dept., World Council of Churches, Geneva).
Augsburg Publishing House, Minneapolis, U.S.A. $4.50.

Institutionalism and Church Unity

A symposium prepared by the Study Commission on Institutionalism, ed. N. Ehrenström and W. G. Meulder.
Association Press, New York, 1963. $6.50.
SCM Press, London. 35s.

Worship and the Acts of God

A symposium prepared by the European Section of the Theological Commission on Worship, ed. W. Vos.
Studia Liturgica Press, Nieuwendam, Netherlands, 1963. $2.00; 14s.

Schrift und Tradition

Untersuchung einer theologischen Kommission, hrsg. K. E. Skydsgaard und L. Vischer.
EVZ Verlag, Zürich, 1963. Sw. Fr. 14.80.

Anglican-Methodist Relations: some institutional factors.

Papers presented to the Study Commission on Institutionalism, ed. W. S. F. Pickering.
Darton, Longman & Todd, London, 1961. 18s.

The Churches and the Canadian Experience

A Faith and Order study of the Christian Tradition, ed. J. W. Grant. Foreword by D. W. Hay.
Ryerson Press, Toronto, 1963. $1.75.

Worship in Scripture and Tradition

A symposium of essays by members of the North American Section of the Theological Commission on Worship, ed. Massey H. Shepherd. Introduction by Joseph A. Sittler.
Oxford University Press, New York and London, 1964. 31s. 6d.

A Documentary History of the Faith and Order Movement, 1927–1963

Edited by Lukas Vischer.
The Bethany Press, St. Louis, Missouri, 1963. $2.